Transport Statistics Report

GW00372454

Vehicle Licensing Statistics 1995

Motor vehicles currently licensed, new registrations, goods vehicle statistics.

Published July 1996

London: HMSO

Brief extracts from this publication may be reproduced provided the source is fully acknowledged. Proposals for the reproduction of larger extracts should be addressed to the HMSO Copyright Unit, St. Clements House, 2-16 Colegate, Norwich NR3 1BQ.

Government Statistical Service

A service of statistical information and advice is provided to the Government by specialist staff employed in individual departments. Statistics are made generally available through their publications and further information and advice on them can be obtained from the Departments concerned.

Enquiries about the contents of this publication should be made to:

Department of Transport
Directorate for Strategy and Analysis
Statistics branch STA2
Room A612
Romney House
43 Marsham Street
London SW1P 3PY
Telephone 0171 276 8818

It is planned that in Autumn 1996 Statistics branch STA2 will relocate to:-

Zone 1/33
Great Minster House
76 Marsham Street
London
SW1P 4DR
Telephone 0171 271 3740

Produced from camera ready copy supplied by the Department of Transport

The price of this publication has been set to contribute to the preparation costs incurred at the Department of Transport

CONTENTS   PAGE

Motor vehicles registered for the first time - historic series

International comparisons of vehicle stock

Goods vehicles statistics

Introduction

This is the 4th edition of "Vehicle Licensing Statistics" and is published in the same basic format as the 1994 edition, with 27 tables, accompanied by commentary and charts.

This edition includes a special supplement to explain the changes in the vehicle taxation system announced in the November 1994 budget and introduced on the 1st July 1995, and the further changes announced in the November 1995 budget, which came into effect on 29th November 1995.

This report is intended to be a comprehensive, relevant and detailed compendium of vehicle licensing statistics. Any suggestions on improvements or additional tables that readers might find useful should be directed to the contact point on the inner front cover.

Derek Jones
Statistician
Department of Transport
Statistics Branch STA2

July 1996

Special supplement: Changes in the vehicle taxation system 1995

A considerable number of changes to the vehicle taxation system were introduced in 1995, with the intention of removing many of the complications in the existing structure. The strategy was to link VED rates for as many vehicles as possible either to the rate for the **private and light goods** group (PLG), or the basic minimum rate for **heavy goods vehicles** (HGVs).

To achieve this, three "umbrella" taxation groups were created:-

An **emergency vehicles group** - exempt from VED.

A **special concessionary group**, including agricultural machines, snow ploughs, gritting vehicles, electric vehicles and, later, steam powered vehicles, paying VED, at current rates, of £35 per annum.

A **special vehicles group**, limited to vehicles over 3500 kgs, including mobile cranes, works trucks, digging machines, showmen's vehicles, etc., paying VED at a rate equivalent to the basic minimum rate for HGVs, currently £150.

In addition, the goods vehicle taxation system was itself considerably simplified by the abolition of separate goods vehicle classes for farmers and showmen. All remaining light goods vehicle taxation classes were also abolished and vehicles in those groups transferred to the PLG class. At the same time, the basis for calculation of excise duty for goods vehicles was amended to "revenue weight". Revenue weight means either "confirmed maximum gross weight" as determined by plating and testing regulations, or "design weight" for vehicles not subject to plating and testing (formerly known as Restricted HGVs).

The process also included further simplifications and "tidying" arrangements. These included cases in which vehicles not over less than 3500 kgs gross weight were moved into the private and light goods taxation class rather than remaining in specialised taxation classes and groups, and the re-allocation of some tax classes into more appropriate groups.

The changes were completed by the introduction of a **new exempt class** in the November 1995 budget for vehicles previously in the private and light goods or motorcycle groups over 25 of years of age.

In general, the process of implementing these changes was gradual, and vehicles were allowed to remain in their current class until a new tax disk was required, whereupon they were transferred into other groups and classes as appropriate.

Since tax disks may run for up to a year, some vehicles remained legitimately taxed in abolished groups at the end of 1995. It is expected that all such vehicles will have transferred into new groups by the end of 1996, but until that process is complete, users of taxation and stock statistics should take special care to ensure they are aware of which classes have been abolished and the processes by which vehicles were re-allocated to other groups.

The attached table gives full detail of all the changes.

Changes to vehicle taxation system: 1995

Changes operative from 1st July 1995.

Tax class	Tax group	Class description	Change	Expected re-allocation of vehicles effected by the change
03	Goods	HGV Farmer's	Abolished	Mainly to class 01-HGV. A few vehicles may transfer to the special concession group as agricultural machines, or fall into class 57 "special types" or class 16 small island goods vehicles.
04	Goods	Trailer HGV Farmer's	Abolished	Mainly to classes 02-Trailer HGV. A few vehicles may transfer to the special concession group as agricultural machines, or fall into class 57 "special types" or class 16-small island goods vehicles.
05	Goods	HGV Showman's	Abolished	To class 14-Special vehicles.
06	Goods	Trailer HGV Showman's	Abolished	To class 15-Special vehicles/special trailer duty.
07	Goods	Restricted HGV	Abolished	Mainly to classes 1-HGV and 2-trailer HGV. A very few vehicles may qualify to transfer into class 16- small island goods vehicles.
08	Goods	Restricted HGV Farmer's	Abolished	Mainly to classes 1-HGV and 2-Trailer HGV. A few vehicles may transfer to the special concession group as agricultural machines, or fall into class 57 "special types" or class 16 small island goods vehicles.
09	Goods	Restricted HGV Showman's	Abolished	To classes 14-Special vehicles, and 15-Special trailer.
20/21/22	PLG group	Light goods Farmer's	Abolished	To class 11-Private and light goods.
29/30	PLG group	Light goods showman's	Abolished	To class 11-Private and light goods.
32	PLG group	Tower wagon	Abolished	Normally to class 01-HGV, but if not over 3500 kgs gross weight to class 11-Private and light goods.
33	PLG group	Trailer tower wagon	Abolished	Normally to class 01-HGV, but if not over 3500 kgs gross weight to class 11-Private and light goods.

Tax class	Tax group	Class description	Change	Expected re-allocation of vehicles effected by the change
35	Hackney	Public transport vehicles	Abolished/ Replaced	Vehicles with 8 or fewer seats to 11-Private and light goods. Vehicles with more than 8 seats to class 34-Bus class.
41	Agricultural and special machines	Digging machines	Abolished	Normally to class 14-Special vehicles, but if not over 3500 kgs gross weight to class 11-Private and light goods.
42	Agricultural and special machines	Mobile cranes	Abolished	Normally to class 14-Special vehicles, but if not over 3500 kgs gross weight to class 11-Private and light goods.
43	Agricultural and special machines	Works trucks	Abolished	Normally to class 14-Special vehicles, but if not over 3500 kgs gross weight to class 11-Private and light goods.
47	Other	Recovery vehicles	Modified	Normally vehicles remain in class 47-recovery, but if not over 3500 kgs gross weight to class 11-Private and light goods.
54	Others	Showman's Haulage	Abolished	To class 14-Special vehicles.
62	Exempt	Exemption under Vehicle Excise Act: Section 7: Under 6 miles per week on public roads.	Abolished	As appropriate for body type, construction and vehicle use. Some may qualify for transfer to class 77- Exempt limited use: for journeys under 1.5kms between keeper's land only.
67	Exempt	Road roller	Abolished	Normally to class 14-special vehicles, but if not over 3500 kgs gross weight to class 11-Private and light goods.
76	Exempt	Police vehicles	New tax class	This class forms part of the "emergency vehicles" umbrella group.
80	Exempt	Road construction	Abolished	If not over 3500 kgs gross weight to class 11-Private and light goods, otherwise to appropriate goods vehicle classes, mainly 01-HGV and 02-Trailer HGV.
81	Exempt	Gritting vehicle	Transfer	Vehicles remain in class 81 but lose exemption and pay VED as part of "special concession" group.

Tax class	Tax group	Class description	Change	Expected re-allocation of vehicles effected by the change
82	Exempt	Snow plough	Transfer	Vehicles remain in class 82 but lose exemption and pay VED as part of "special concession" group.
83	Exempt	Street lighting	Abolished	Normally to appropriate goods vehicle classes, mainly 01-HGV and 02-Trailer HGV, but if not over 3500 kgs gross weight to class 11-Private and light goods.
84	Exempt	Street cleansing	Abolished	Normally to appropriate goods vehicle classes, mainly 01-HGV and 02-Trailer HGV, but if not over 3500 kgs gross weight to class 11-Private and light goods.

Changes operative from 29th November 1995.

Tax class	Tax group	Class description	Change	Expected re-allocation of vehicles effected by the change
10	Private and light goods	Private use HGV	New tax class	This class identifies goods vehicles over 3500 kgs gross weight used exclusively for private purposes. Previously these vehicles were included in class 11-Private and light goods and paid VED accordingly. Vehicles now pay minimum flat rate for HGVs. Vehicles in this group must not be used for commercial, trade or business purposes.
19	Motorcycles	Electric motorcycles and tricycles	New tax class	New class for electrically powered motorcycles and tricycles. Vehicles must not exceed 450kgs.
37	Special concession	Steam propelled	New tax class	Forms part of the "special concession" group.
79 (26/27)	Exempt	Electric with Goods (electric) and Trailer goods (electric)	Transfer	To class 79-Electric, but loses previous exemption and now included in "special concession" group and pay VED accordingly.
87	Exempt	NHS vehicle	New tax class	Technical change to assist distinction between various types of exempt vehicles including NHS emergency, and other crown vehicles.
88	Private and light goods and Motorcycles	Exemption vehicle over 25 years old	New tax class	Exemption available to all vehicles over 25 years of age previously taxed in Private and light goods and motorcycle groups.

Commentary and charts

Licensed vehicle stock 1985-1995

- The **total vehicle stock in Great Britain** at the end of 1995 was estimated to be 25.37 million vehicles, of which 21.39 million vehicles, or about 84%, were motorcars. The next most numerous vehicle group by <u>body type</u> was light goods vehicles with a stock of over 1.95 million vehicles, or roughly 7.5% of the total.

- The **remainder of the stock** is made up of 702,000 motorcycles; 556,000 other goods vehicles; 280,000 agricultural tractors; 150,000 buses and coaches; 30,000 three wheelers; 30,000 custom built taxis; and 270,000 other assorted vehicle types. Note that a vehicle's body type is not always a reliable guide to its taxation class, for example, of the above 150,000 buses about half are licensed for public use, the bulk of the remainder being minibuses taxed for private use.

- The final group of 270,000 other assorted vehicle types includes emergency service vehicles such as fire engines and ambulances, road repair vehicles such as road surfacers, road surface strippers, bulldozers, tar sprayers, road rollers and line painters, road maintenance vehicles such as street cleansing, snow ploughs and gritting lorries and various types of construction vehicles, cranes, shovels, diggers and excavators.

- The **total stock of vehicles has grown** by an estimated 21.2% between the end of 1985 and the end of 1995; a rate equivalent to 1.95% per annum. Growth has been lower in recent years. Since the end of 1990, the estimated total growth in vehicle stock is 4.0%; a rate equivalent to 0.78% per annum.

- **Growth in motorcar stock** totalled 28.6% between 1985 and 1995, equivalent to 2.54% per annum, and totalled 7.0% between 1990 and 1995 equivalent to 1.36% per annum..

- The stock of vehicles with **goods body types** remained relatively constant between 1985 and 1987, grew by about 6.0% between the end of 1987 and the end of 1989, and has since declined. The stock at the end of 1995 was 556,000 vehicles, an estimated overall reduction of 11.3% since 1985, and a reduction of 16.7% since the 1989 peak.

- **Motorcycle stocks** have declined steadily over the last ten years, by an estimated 44% in total, a rate equivalent to 5.6% fewer vehicles per year. The overall reduction of more than 560,000 motorcycles helps explain why total vehicle stocks have grown more slowly than motorcar stocks.

Licensed vehicle stock 1985-95: By body type

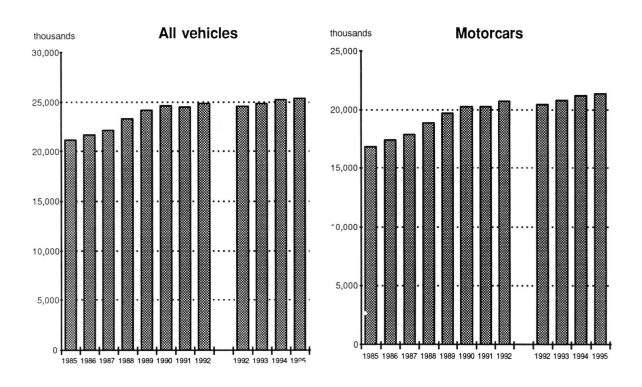

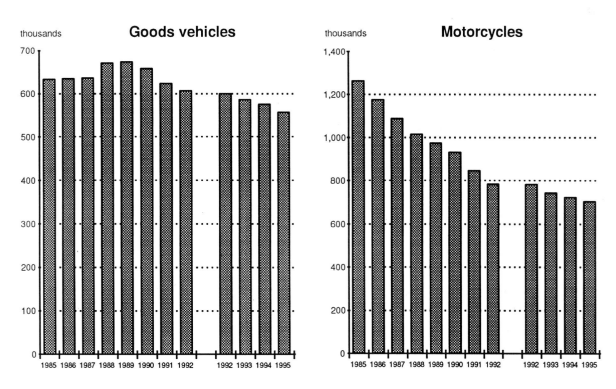

Source: 1985-1992 DVLA Annual Vehicle Census
Source: 1992-1995 DOT Vehicle Information Database

Vehicles registered for the first time 1985 to 1995

- In the past ten years, **new vehicle registrations** have ranged between a maximum of 2.83 million vehicles in 1989 and a minimum of 1.90 million vehicles in 1992. Registrations in 1995, at 2.31 million, were 2.5% higher than the figure for the previous year, and at an almost identical level to the 1985 total.

- **Registrations of new motorcars** followed a similar pattern, with a maximum of 2.30 million cars in 1989 and a minimum of 1.60 million cars in both 1991 and 1992. Registrations in 1995, at 1.94 million, were 5.2% higher than in 1985. Between 1985 and 1995 the proportion of new vehicles registered to a keeper with a company title has increased from 45% to 52%, while the residue, registered to private keepers has reduced by the corresponding amount. Most of the increase occurred between 1985 and 1988, and since 1988 company registrations have been fairly steady at between 51% and 53%.

- **Since the end of 1985** a total of 23.25 million new vehicles have been registered, while stocks have grown by an estimated 4.49 million. For cars, 19.24 million new cars have been registered, while stocks have grown by an estimated 4.80 million. So roughly 4 in every 5 new vehicles, and roughly 3 in every 4 new cars have replaced existing stocks rather than added to the vehicle population.

- New vehicles registered in **goods vehicle taxation classes** also reached their maximum in 1989 with 65 thousand new registrations, but the minimum was in 1991 with 29 thousand new registrations. The relative gap between these high and low points was much greater than for other vehicle types. Registrations in 1995 at 48 thousand vehicles were 17% higher than in 1994, but 7% below the 1985 figure and 26% below the 1989 peak.

- Although registrations of **new motorcycles** showed little change between 1987 and 1988 and have even increased in some years (1989, 1994 and 1995) registrations have shown a considerable overall decline in the ten year period from 1985. The number of new motorcycles registered in 1995 at 68.9 thousand was nearly 6.7% higher than the figure for 1984, but still 45% lower than in 1985. Whilst, in part, this may reflect consumer choice, motorcycle driving tests have also become more difficult and learner motorcyclists subject to additional regulations as the government, as part of its road safety policy, has tried to reduce the number of motorcyclists killed and injured on Britain's roads.

- In 1982 two part motorcycle tests were introduced and provisional motorcycle licenses restricted to two years. In 1983 learner motorcyclists were only allowed to ride machines up to 125 cc's. In 1989 accompanied motorcycle testing became mandatory. In 1990 compulsory basic training for learner motorcyclists was introduced, and learner motorcyclists were banned from carrying pillion passengers.

Vehicles registered for the first time: 1985-95

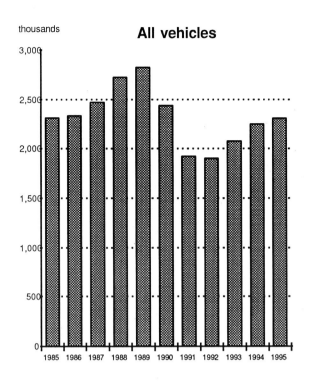

thousands

All vehicles

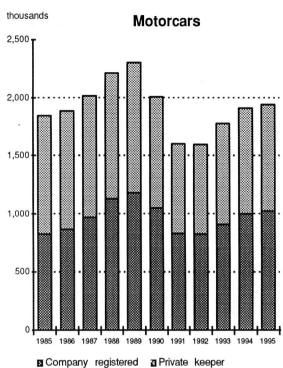

thousands

Motorcars

■ Company registered ▨ Private keeper

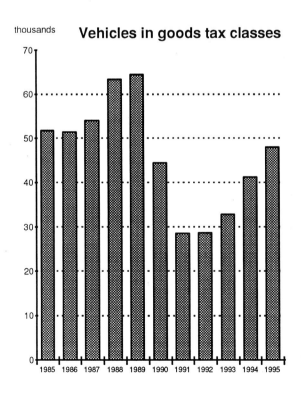

thousands

Vehicles in goods tax classes

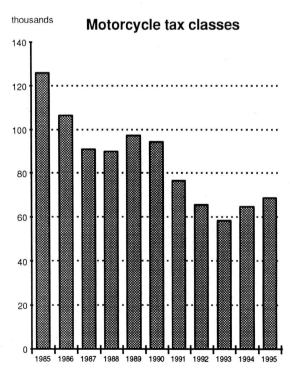

thousands

Motorcycle tax classes

Vehicle details: 1985 and 1995 compared

-    The taxation group "hackney" for **public transport vehicles**, which covered both taxis and buses and coaches, was abolished from end of June 1995, and replaced with a new "bus" taxation group covering only vehicles with more than 8 seats. Vehicles were not automatically transferred to the new tax class, but re-allocated on renewal of their vehicle excise duty tax disk. By the end of 1995 vehicles there were still some eight thousand vehicles with 8 or fewer seats remaining in the old class.

-    Comparisons between 1985 and 1995 for vehicles with 8 or fewer seats are not meaningful, and only vehicles with 9 or more are included in the graphs on the opposite page. The group having 9 to 32 seats, which includes minibuses and smaller buses and coaches has increased from 14% to 32% of bus stocks, while the proportion of larger buses and coaches, that is with 48 or more seats has declined from 73% to 56% of stocks.

-    The greatest change in the composition of **goods vehicle stock** between 1985 and 1995 has been the marked increase in the proportion of vehicles in the gross weight range from 33 to 38 tonnes, probably as a result of changes in regulations introduced in May 1983 which increased the maximum gross vehicle weight limit from 32.5 tonnes to 38 tonnes. This increase, and a slight increase in the proportion of lorries in the gross weight range up to 7.5 tonnes (vehicles which can be driven on an ordinary driving licence) is mirrored by a general fall in the proportion of general goods vehicles in other weight ranges.

-    As the section on licensed stock showed, the **overall stock of motorcycles** has roughly halved between 1985 and 1995. Accompanying this change in numbers has been a marked upward shift in the average engine capacity of bikes in use. The proportion having engine capacities up to 50 cc's has fallen by about 17 percentage points, whereas the proportion with capacities over 500 cc's has not only increased from less than 10% to over 30% of licensed stock, but has also doubled in absolute terms from 98,000 to 196,000 bikes.

-    **Vehicles subject to one or more forms of exemption** of vehicle excise duty have increased from 695,000 in 1985 to 1,169,000 in 1995. At the end of 1995 120,000 of these vehicles qualified for exemption under the "older than 25 years" rule introduced in the November 1995 budget. The largest single group of exempt vehicles are those owned by disabled drivers, which make up 61% of the 1995 total compared with 33% of the total in 1985. Crown vehicles have almost halved from 39,000 to 20,000 over the ten year period. Exempt vehicles overall have increased from 3.3% of total stock to 4.6% of total licensed stock between 1985 and 1995.

-    More detailed comparisons of motorcars, particularly changes in engine capacity, are given in the section specific to that group.

Vehicle details: 1985 and 1995 compared

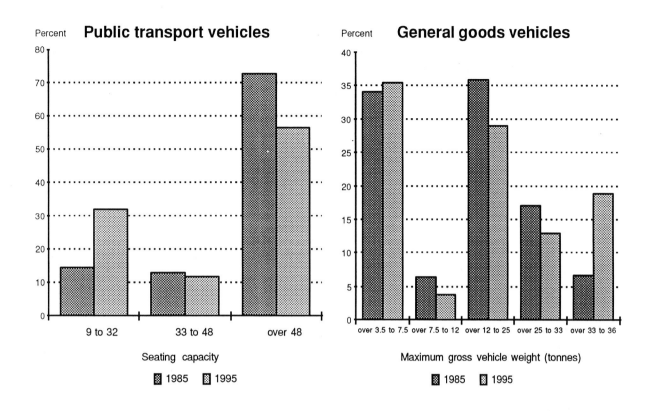

Public transport vehicles

Percent

Seating capacity

■ 1985　■ 1995

General goods vehicles

Percent

Maximum gross vehicle weight (tonnes)

■ 1985　■ 1995

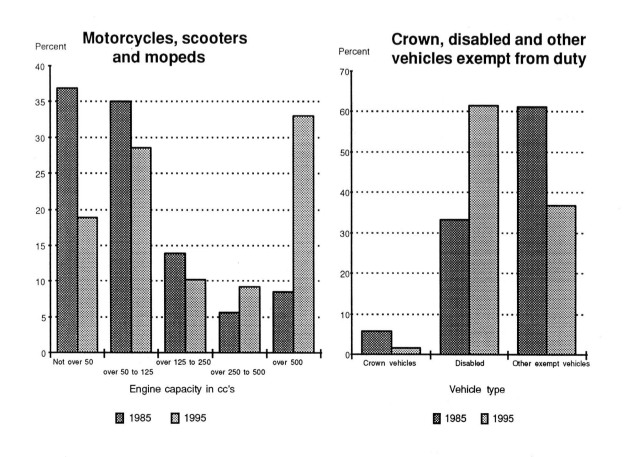

Motorcycles, scooters and mopeds

Percent

Engine capacity in cc's

■ 1985　■ 1995

Crown, disabled and other vehicles exempt from duty

Percent

Vehicle type

■ 1985　■ 1995

Current vehicle stock: Year of first registration

-       Very few vehicles are not new when first registered. For all practical purposes therefore the **year of first registration** can be used to monitor the age of any sample of vehicles. For example, vehicles first registered in 1995 will, in general, be not more than one year old by the end of that year, vehicles first registered in 1994 not more than two years old at the end of 1995, etc. etc.

-       The age profile of most vehicles types reflects the peak in new registration which occurred in 1989. Despite wastage, the group of **motorcars** registered in 1989 remains the largest at almost 9.5% of licensed stock. Of currently licensed motorcars nearly 17% are not more than two years old, but nearly 2% were registered before 1979, and are now at least 17 years old.

-       Among the common vehicle types, **public transport vehicles** (vehicles with more than 8 seats only) have the largest group of old vehicles, with about 12% registered before 1979, and now at least 17 years old. Other age groups are roughly evenly distributed, albeit with some peaking in the 1986 to 1989 period.

-       Although **motorcycles** are generally among the most short lived of all vehicles, older bikes were registered in substantially greater numbers than in recent years. For example, in 1980 and 1981 a combined total of over 570,000 new bikes were registered compared with a combined total of 133,500 in 1994 and 1995. Despite wastage, substantial numbers of these older bikes remain in the currently licensed stock so that even vehicles registered in 1980 still make up nearly 4% of current stocks.

-       Currently licensed **goods vehicles** show a marked peak in 1988 and 1989 when registrations were very high. The proportion of vehicles registered in these two years forming 11% and 12% respectively of currently licensed stock. Under 1% of goods vehicles were registered before 1979, and 21% were registered within the last two years. Goods vehicles over 38 tonnes gross weight can only be used for combined transport operations and almost all registrations over this weight have been in 1995.

Current vehicle stock: Year of 1st registration

Motorcars: PLG taxation group

Percent

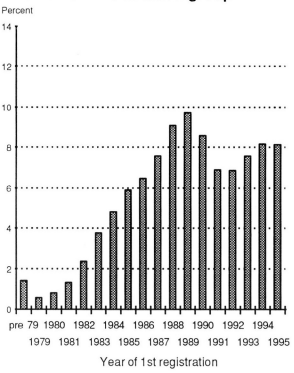

Year of 1st registration

Public transport vehicles: 9 or more seats

Percent

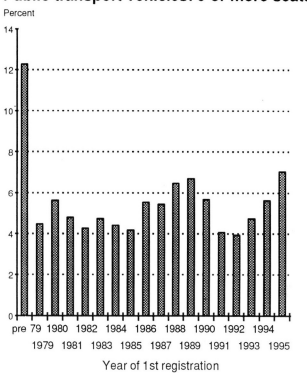

Year of 1st registration

General goods vehicles

Percent

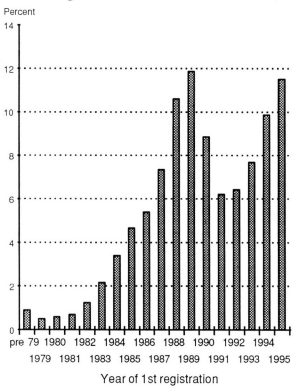

Year of 1st registration

Motorcycles, scooters and mopeds

Percent

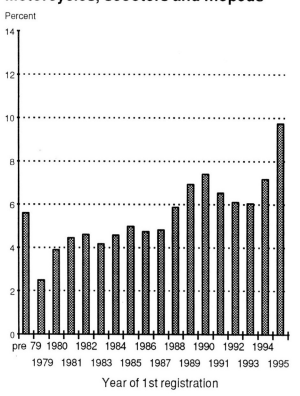

Year of 1st registration

Goods vehicle stock 1995

-        Tables 18 onwards in this report give details of the currently licensed "**goods vehicle stock**". Although tabulations giving information on vehicles in goods vehicle taxation classes, and having goods vehicle construction are useful, they have some disadvantages.

-        For example, some special vehicles may be in goods vehicle taxation groups and weigh less than 3,500 kgs, which would normally result in being taxed in the Private and Light Goods group. Moreover, some heavy goods vehicles may be taxed in other groups.

-        Tables 18 onwards give statistics for a carefully defined set of currently licensed goods vehicles, all of which exceed 3,500 kgs maximum gross vehicle weight. The vehicles included are all those in taxation groups 1 to 9 (the most common heavy goods vehicle taxation groups) plus vehicles with goods vehicle body types in electric taxation groups, crown vehicles and other exempt classes provided they have goods vehicle body types.

-        The goods vehicle stock, defined in this way, stood at 418,000 vehicles at the end of 1993, of which 311,000 were rigid vehicles and 107,000 articulated. This is a slight rise of 0.5% on 1994 and is the second year to show an increase following a period of decline from the 1989 peak of 478,000 vehicles.

-        Many goods vehicles are constructed to maximise the amount of goods that can be carried within regulations and taxation bands. **Rigid 2 axle goods vehicles** cannot exceed 17 tonnes, **rigid 3 axle goods vehicles** cannot exceed 24.39 tonnes and rigid 4 axle goods cannot exceed 30.49 tonnes. The maximum weight for **4 axle articulated** goods vehicles is 33 tonnes, and for **5 axle articulated** goods vehicles 38 tonnes. **Articulated vehicles with 6 axles** are permitted a maximum gross vehicle weight of up to 44 tonnes provided they are engaged in Combined Transport operations only. The maximum weight vehicle that can be driven on an ordinary driving license in 7.5 tonnes.

-        Two axle vehicles remain the most common form of rigid lorry. Two axle articulated tractor units outnumber 3 axle units by more than two to one. Most articulated tractors are licensed to pull either 3 axle trailers, or any axle trailer configuration. Articulated vehicle **trailers** do not need to be registered with DVLA and are not subject to vehicle excise duty. They are, however, subject to Vehicle Inspectorate roadworthiness tests, and from this source, the total stock in 1994 is estimated at roughly 226,000 trailers.

Goods vehicle stock 1995: Weight & axle details

Rigid vehicles

Articulated vehicles

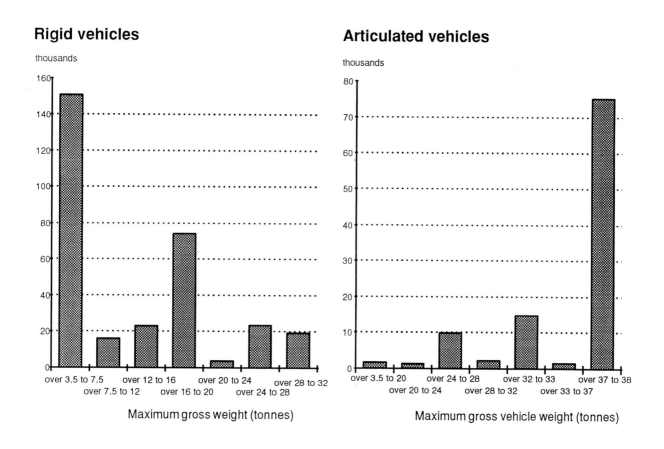

Rigid vehicles

Articulated vehicles

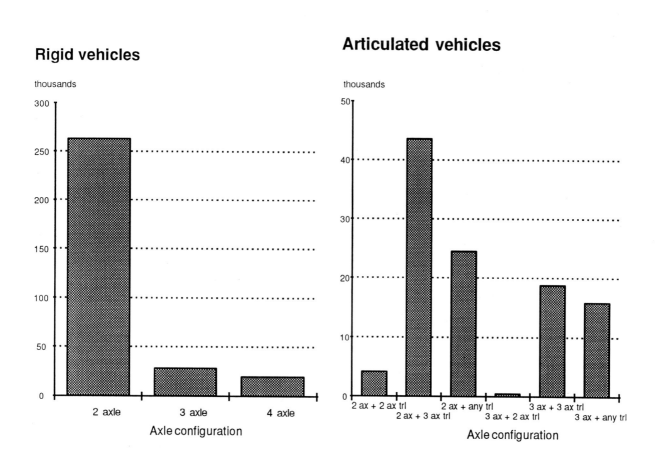

15

Currently licensed motorcars: Vehicle details

- At the end of 1995 there were some 21.39 million vehicles with **car body** types licensed to use GB roads. Of these, an overwhelming majority, 20.51 million cars, were taxed within the private and light goods taxation group. Most of the rest were taxed within the group of exempt vehicles, claiming exemption in the disabled driver category, but since November 1995 some 0.12 million are claiming exemption for being more than 25 years old.

- The title code of the **registered vehicle keeper** showed that 2.23 million cars, or 10.4% of the total, were registered as company owned.

- At the end of 1995, some 8.8% of currently licensed motorcars were **diesel** propelled, though just under 7% of vehicle registered to private keepers are diesel propelled vehicles, compared with the 25% of cars registered to companies that are diesel propelled. However, companies tend to own and use newer cars than private keepers. This difference may fall as time passes, and increasing numbers of diesel driven company cars come onto the second hand market. Modern cars are almost exclusively propelled by diesel or petrol, only 0.01% being electrically or otherwise propelled.

- The **engine capacity** of petrol driven motorcars is, on average, lower than that for diesel driven cars. Only 0.4% of diesel driven cars have engines smaller than 1200 cc's, whereas 9.7% of petrol driven cars have engine capacities less than 1000 cc's. Nevertheless, diesel cars have better fuel consumption figures (that is more miles per gallon of fuel) than petrol driven cars. In other espects, diesel powered cars produce much lower emissions of carbon monoxide, hydrocardons, and oxides of nitrogen than petrol powered cars, but much higher emissions of particulates (smoke).

Currently licensed motorcars: Vehicle details

Taxation class

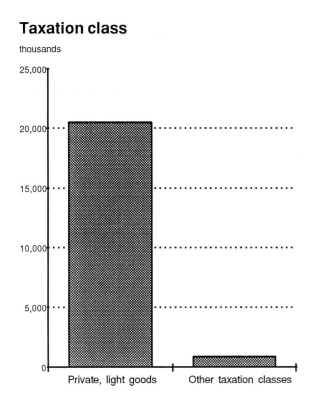

Registered keeper/propulsion

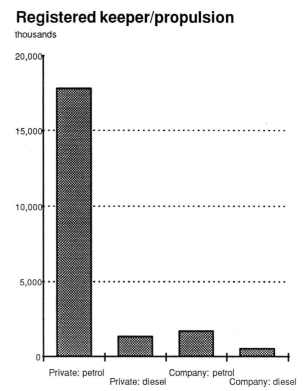

Engine capacity: petrol propulsion

Engine capacity: diesel propulsion

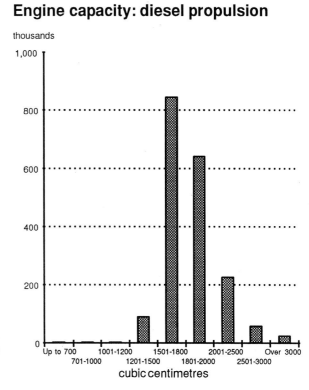

Table 1 Motor vehicles currently licensed: by taxation group: 1985-95[1]

Thousands

| | Private and light goods[2] | | | Public transportation | | | | |
| | | | Motor cycles scooters and mopeds | Hackney taxation class[3] | *of which:* Bus taxation class[4] | Goods[6] | Special machines/ Special concession[7] | Other vehicles[8] |
Year	Body type cars	Other vehicles						
1985	16,454	1,805	1,148	120	67 [5]	485	374	78
1986	16,981	1,880	1,065	125	68 [5]	484	371	73
1987	17,421	1,952	978	129	71 [5]	485	374	68
1988	18,432	2,096	912	132	73 [5]	502	383	83
1989	19,248	2,199	875	122	73 [5]	505	384	77
1990	19,742	2,247	833	115	73 [5]	482	375	71
1991	19,737	2,215	750	109	72 [5]	449	346	65
1992	20,116	2,228	688	108	73 [5]	437	324	59
1992	19,870	2,198	684	107	72 [5]	432	324	59
1993	20,102	2,187	650	107	73 [5]	428	318	55
1994	20,479	2,192	630	107	75 [5]	434	309	50
1995	20,505	2,217	594	..	74	421	274	44

continued

| | | | | body type cars in all taxation classes | | | | |
| | | | | | | *of which:* | | |
Year	Crown and exempt	Special vehicles group	All vehicles	All body type cars	Company	Diesel	Per cent company	Per cent diesel
1985	695		21,159	16,829	1,981	176	*11.8*	*1.0*
1986	720		21,699	17,389	2,038	245	*11.7*	*1.4*
1987	744		22,152	17,856	2,170	352	*12.2*	*2.0*
1988	761		23,302	18,888	2,391	418	*12.7*	*2.2*
1989	785		24,196	19,720	2,579	528	*13.0*	*2.7*
1990	807		24,673	20,230	2,613	638	*12.9*	*3.2*
1991	840		24,511	20,253	2,435	751	*12.0*	*3.7*
1992	891		24,851	20,681	2,321	931	*11.2*	*4.5*
1992	903		24,577	20,444	2,272	920	*11.1*	*4.5*
1993	979		24,826	20,755	2,221	1,226	*10.7*	*5.9*
1994	1,030		25,231	21,199	2,197	1,576	*10.4*	*7.4*
1995	1,169	28 [9]	25,369 [10]	21,394	2,231	1,891	*10.4*	*8.8*

1 See supplement on recent taxation class changes, and also notes and definitions.

2 For years up to 1990 retrospective counts within these new taxation classes have been estimated.

3 Taxation class 35, Hackney. Public transportation vehicles including taxis: Abolished 30th June 1995

4 Taxation class 34, Buses. Public transportation vehicles with more than 8 seats. Introduced 1st July 1995.

5 Estimated: Retrospective estimates are based on vehicles registrations in tax class 35, with more than 8 seats

6 Until 30th June 1995 included agricultural vans and lorries and showman's goods vehicles licensed to draw trailers. From 1st July 1995 separate taxation groups for farmers and showmen were abolished.

7 The agricultural and special machines taxation group was abolished on 30th June 1995 and replaced by the special concession taxation group from 1st July 1995. See supplement.

8 Includes three wheelers, general haulage and others.

9 Special vehicles group: Introduced 1st July 1995: See supplement

10 Contains 44,000 vehicles still taxed in abolished taxation classes

Table 2 Motor vehicles currently licensed: vehicle details: 1985-95 [1]

(a) Private and light goods: [2] Body type cars within private and light goods by engine size | | | | | | | | | | | | | Thousands

Over	Not over	1985	1986	1987	1988	1989	1990	1991	1992	1992	1993	1994	1995
	700cc	123	120	114	108	99	90	79	71	70	62	54	46
700cc	1,000cc	1,891	1,963	2,022	2,145	2,205	2,215	2,163	2,109	2,084	1,998	1,905	1,757
1,000cc	1,200cc	2,128	2,153	2,154	2,201	2,215	2,226	2,198	2,232	2,207	2,227	2,261	2,258
1,200cc	1,500cc	5,076	5,115	5,111	5,259	5,361	5,418	5,358	5,411	5,349	5,330	5,337	5,225
1,500cc	1,800cc	4,278	4,573	4,850	5,279	5,641	5,872	5,944	6,105	6,025	6,129	6,276	6,345
1,800cc	2,000cc	1,556	1,616	1,718	1,920	2,162	2,352	2,465	2,655	2,622	2,841	3,088	3,274
2,000cc	2,500cc	665	694	710	736	747	744	726	727	719	722	759	791
2,500cc	3,000cc	433	445	448	476	501	509	498	496	489	482	486	494
3,000cc		301	301	294	307	314	. 315	306	309	305	312	313	315
cc not known		2	1	1	1	1	1	1	-	-	-	-	-
All capacities		16,454	16,981	17,421	18,432	19,248	19,742	19,740	20,116	19,870	20,102	20,479	20,505
Other vehicles		1,805	1,880	1,952	2,095	2,199	2,247	2,215	2,230	2,198	2,187	2,192	2,217
All PLG		18,259	18,259	19,374	20,528	21,447	21,989	21,952	22,345	22,069	22,289	22,672	22,722

(b) Motor cycles, scooters and mopeds: by engine size | | | | | | | | | | | | | Thousands

Over	Not over	1985	1986	1987	1988	1989	1990	1991	1992	1992	1993	1994	1995
	50cc	423	389	352	312	280	248	207	174	173	147	129	112
50cc	125cc	402	377	347	320	303	284	249	221	222	204	187	170
125cc	150cc	6	5	4	3	3	3	2	2	2	2	2	1
150cc	200cc	54	45	39	34	31	28	24	21	22	19	18	14
200cc	250cc	99	88	78	71	68	65	60	55	55	52	50	46
250cc	350cc	12	13	13	15	16	16	15	15	15	15	15	12
350cc	500cc	53	49	46	45	45	45	42	42	41	42	45	43
500cc		98	98	99	112	131	146	150	158	155	169	186	196
All over 50cc		725	676	626	600	595	587	543	514	512	503	502	482
All engine sizes		1,148	1,065	978	912	875	835	750	688	684	650	630	594

(c) Public transport vehicles: by seating capacity | | | | | | | | | | | | | Thousands

Over	Not over	1985	1986	1987	1988	1989	1990	1991	1992	1992	1993	1994	1995
	4 seats	43.7	47.0	47.7	46.7	35.3	26.8	21.5	18.1	18.0	15.4	13.3	2.6
4 seats	8 seats	9.3	9.6	10.5	13.0	14.0	15.0	16.1	17.1	17.0	17.9	19.2	5.5
All 8 seats or less		53.0	56.6	58.2	59.7	49.3	42.0	37.6	35.3	35.0	33.4	32.5	8.0
8 seats	32 seats	9.6	12.3	15.3	17.3	18.9	20.0	20.7	21.5	21.4	22.5	23.2	23.5
32 seats	48 seats	8.6	8.0	7.7	7.3	6.7	6.3	6.1	6.4	6.4	6.8	7.8	8.6
48 seats		48.6	48.0	47.9	48.2	47.3	46.2	44.8	44.6	44.4	43.9	43.5	41.6
All over 8 seats		66.8	68.4	70.8	72.8	72.9	72.5	71.5	72.5	72.2	73.3	74.5	73.8
All capacities		119.8	125.0	129.0	132.5	122.2	114.7	109.1	107.8	107.2	106.6	107.0	..

(d) General goods: by gross weight | | | | | | | | | | | | | Thousands

Over	Not over	1985	1986	1987	1988	1989	1990	1991	1992	1992	1993	1994	1995
3.5 tonnes	7.5 tonnes	138	141	145	153	157	155	148	143	143	139	139	144
7.5 tonnes	12 tonnes	26	24	22	21	20	18	17	16	16	15	15	15
12 tonnes	25 tonnes	145	143	143	147	146	140	129	124	123	120	118	118
25 tonnes	33 tonnes	69	66	64	65	62	55	49	46	45	47	51	52
33 tonnes	38 tonnes	27	34	41	51	59	61	60	63	62	65	71	76
38 tonnes		-	-	-	-	-	-	-	-	-	-	-	1
Gross wt unknown		7	7	7	7	7	2	1	1	1	-	-	-
All vehicles		412	415	422	444	451	432	403	393	389	387	394	406

1 The vehicle taxation system was subject to major revisions in 1995: See supplement.
2 Counts of vehicles in 'Private and light goods' have been estimated up to 1991.

19

Table 2 (continued) Motor vehicles currently licensed: vehicle details: 1985-95

(e) Farmers' goods: by gross weight/Abolished - vehicles will move to other groups on renewal of tax disk. Thousands

Over	Not over	1985	1986	1987	1988	1989	1990	1991	1992	1992	1993	1994	1995
	3.5 tonnes	3	22	21	19	18	20	20	19	19	19	20	7
3.5 tonnes	7.5 tonnes	8	8	7	7	7	7	7	7	7	6	6	2
7.5 tonnes	12 tonnes	2	2	2	2	2	1	1	1	1	1	1	-
12 tonnes	25 tonnes	7	7	6	6	5	4	5	5	5	4	4	2
25 tonnes	33 tonnes	2	1	1	1	1	1	1	1	1	1	1	-
33 tonnes	38 tonnes	-	-	-	-	-	1	1	1	1	1	1	-
38 tonnes		-	-	-	-	-	-	-	-	-	-	-	-
Gross weight unknow		51	28	25	23	20	14	12	10	10	8	7	2
All vehicles		73	68	62	58	54	48	46	43	43	41	40	15

(f) Special machines/special concession group (Mainly agricultural tractors and machinery) Thousands

	1985	1986	1987	1988	1989	1990	1991	1992	1992	1993	1994	1995
Agricultural tractors	247	244	245	246	241	237	221	209	210	207	202	203
Combine harvesters and other agric. machinery	42	42	42	43	43	44	41	40	40	40	40	44
Mowing machines	11	11	11	12	12	11	8	7	7	7	6	6
Electric												16
Gritting vehicle												3
Snow plough												1
Steam vehicles												
All vehicles	374	371	374	383	384	376	346	324	324	318	309	274

(g) Other licensed vehicles Thousands

	1985	1986	1987	1988	1989	1990	1991	1992	1992	1993	1994	1995
Three wheelers less than 450 kgs	72	67	62	57	53	48	43	39	39	35	32	29
General haulage [3]	6	6	6	6	5	4	3	2	2	2	2	2
Others	-	-	1	20	20	20	19	18	18	17	15	
Recovery												13
All vehicles	78	73	68	83	77	72	65	59	59	55	50	44

(h) Crown and other vehicles exempt from licence duty Thousands

	1985	1986	1987	1988	1989	1990	1991	1992	1992	1993	1994	1995
Crown vehicles	39	39	39	38	38	38	36	35	36	34	34	20
Other exempt:												
Disabled	232	265	296	323	353	385	421	477	483	571	643	718
Over 25 years old												120
Others	424	416	410	399	394	385	383	379	384	374	353	312
All other exempt	656	681	706	722	747	770	804	855	867	945	996	1150
All exempt vehicles	695	721	744	761	785	808	840	891	903	979	1030	1169

(i) Special vehicles group: Tax class 14 and 15 Thousands

	1985	1986	1987	1988	1989	1990	1991	1992	1992	1993	1994	1995
Special vehicles group												28

(j) Other abolished tax groups/Vehicles will transfer to other tax groups on renewal of tax disk.

	1985	1986	1987	1988	1989	1990	1991	1992	1992	1993	1994	1995
Digging machines	37	37	39	42	44	43	40	36	36	35	34	17
Mobile cranes	9	9	8	9	9	9	8	7	7	7	6	3
Works trucks	27	28	29	32	34	32	29	25	25	23	21	13

3 Until end June 1995 also included showman's haulage.

Table 3 Motor vehicles currently licensed: by body type: 1985-1995

Thousands

Year	Cars	Taxis[1]	Motor cycles	Three wheelers	Light goods	Goods	Buses and coaches	Agricultural vehicles etc[2]	Other vehicles[3]	All vehicles
1985	16,829	25	1,262	62	1,606	633	148	344	248	21,157
1986	17,389	26	1,176	60	1,670	634	149	340	256	21,699
1987	17,856	28	1,086	57	1,732	636	150	340	267	22,152
1988	18,888	29	1,016	54	1,863	671	155	341	286	23,302
1989	19,720	30	976	51	1,956	674	156	334	298	24,196
1990	20,230	32	932	47	1,994	658	157	328	297	24,673
1991	20,253	32	848	43	1,961	624	154	309	287	24,511
1992[4]	20,681	32	784	40	1,976	606	155	297	280	24,851
1992[5]	20,444	32	780	40	1,951	600	154	298	280	24,577
1993	20,755	32	744	36	1,943	587	153	294	282	24,826
1994	21,199	32	721	34	1,951	575	154	285	281	25,231
1995	21,394	33	702	31	1,949	556	153	282	268	25,369

1 These include mainly custom built `black cab' design vehicles.

2 Includes various types of harvesters, works trucks, mobile cranes and mowing machines.

3 Examples include ambulances, fire engines, road rollers, road construction vehicles, street cleansing etc etc.

4 For the years up to 1992 estimates are taken from the annual vehicle census based upon DVLA main vehicle file.

5 From 1992 estimates of licensed stock are taken from the Department of Transport's Statistics Directorate Vehicle Information Database.

Table 4 Motor vehicles currently licensed 1995: By year of first registration

(a) Private and light goods: Body type cars within private and light goods by engine size — Thousands

Over	Not over	Pre 1979	1979	1980	1981	1982	1983	1984	1985	1986
	700cc	1.3	0.8	0.7	1.4	2.5	2.6	2.9	4.2	5.7
700cc	1,000cc	29.8	16.2	23.1	54.6	67.7	102.9	125.8	142.8	156.5
1,000cc	1,200cc	30.0	20.8	28.5	41.2	75.6	103.8	137.3	148.2	148.2
1,200cc	1,500cc	70.1	27.2	49.1	79.4	144.1	225.5	280.9	324.4	345.1
1,500cc	1,800cc	48.5	17.5	26.6	47.4	121.4	215.0	285.6	392.4	438.8
1,800cc	2,000cc	20.6	10.5	13.5	19.2	40.2	72.1	88.8	117.6	133.7
2,000cc	2,500cc	16.3	9.4	11.4	17.1	26.7	38.9	44.4	47.2	53.7
2,500cc	3,000cc	14.1	5.8	6.1	7.6	15.5	23.7	24.6	27.8	28.1
3,000cc		23.9	5.4	6.0	6.9	8.5	10.9	12.9	15.5	14.3
cc not known		-	-	-	-	-	-	-	-	-
All capacities		254.7	113.6	165.1	274.8	502.2	795.5	1,003.3	1,220.1	1,324.2
Other vehicles		68.0	15.1	19.1	22.0	36.1	61.2	86.6	120.0	145.2
All PLG		322.7	128.7	184.2	296.8	538.3	856.7	1,089.9	1,340.1	1,469.4

(b) Motor cycles, scooters and mopeds: by engine size — Thousands

Over	Not over	Pre 1979	1979	1980	1981	1982	1983	1984	1985	1986
	50cc	3.5	1.8	3.1	5.1	7.3	6.9	8.2	9.3	8.0
50cc	125cc	7.2	3.2	4.4	4.9	7.8	9.5	11.1	12.0	11.3
125cc	150cc	0.3	-	-	-	-	-	-	-	-
150cc	200cc	2.6	1.2	2.0	2.2	1.0	0.6	0.5	0.4	0.2
200cc	250cc	3.9	2.9	6.0	5.9	4.0	1.4	0.9	0.7	0.8
250cc	350cc	0.5	-	0.2	0.5	0.3	0.3	0.4	0.5	0.8
350cc	500cc	4.6	1.8	2.7	2.6	2.6	1.5	1.1	1.3	1.2
500cc		10.5	3.8	4.5	5.1	4.4	4.5	5.2	5.3	5.6
All over 50cc		29.7	13.1	19.9	21.2	20.0	17.8	19.1	20.3	20.0
All engine sizes		33.2	14.8	23.1	26.3	27.3	24.7	27.2	29.6	28.1

(c) Public transport vehicles: by seating capacity — Thousands

Over	Not over	Pre 1979	1979	1980	1981	1982	1983	1984	1985	1986
	4 seats	0.2	-	0.1	0.2	0.2	0.2	0.2	0.3	0.4
4 seats	8 seats	-	-	-	-	-	-	-	-	-
All 8 seats or less		0.3	0.1	0.1	0.2	0.2	0.2	0.3	0.3	0.5
8 seats	32 seats	0.2	-	0.1	0.2	0.2	0.4	0.4	0.9	2.3
32 seats	48 seats	1.3	0.5	0.3	0.2	0.2	0.3	0.2	0.2	0.1
48 seats		7.5	2.8	3.8	3.1	2.7	2.9	2.7	2.0	1.6
All over 8 seats		9.1	3.3	4.2	3.5	3.2	3.5	3.3	3.1	4.1
All capacities		9.3	3.4	4.3	3.7	3.4	3.7	3.6	3.4	4.6

(d) General goods: by gross weight — Thousands

Over	Not over	Pre 1979	1979	1980	1981	1982	1983	1984	1985	1986
3.5 tonnes	7.5 tonnes	1.8	1.0	1.2	1.5	2.3	3.6	5.2	7.7	8.4
7.5 tonnes	12 tonnes	0.5	0.1	0.2	0.2	0.3	0.4	0.6	0.8	1.0
12 tonnes	25 tonnes	1.0	0.6	0.8	0.8	1.7	3.2	5.0	6.2	7.3
25 tonnes	33 tonnes	0.2	0.2	0.2	0.2	0.4	0.8	1.3	1.7	2.3
33 tonnes	38 tonnes	-	-	-	0.1	0.3	0.8	1.8	2.5	3.0
38 tonnes		-	-	-	-	-	-	-	-	-
Gross weight unknown		-	-	-	-	-	-	-	-	-
All vehicles		3.6	2.0	2.5	2.8	5.0	8.8	13.9	19.0	22.0

Table 4 (continued)

(a) Private and light goods: Body type cars within private and light goods by engine size   Thousands

Over	Not over	1987	1988	1989	1990	1991	1992	1993	1994	1995	All years
	700cc	6.2	5.3	3.9	1.8	0.9	1.0	1.4	1.8	1.4	46.0
700cc	1,000cc	175.2	205.3	177.7	135.3	91.3	55.8	64.1	68.2	64.3	1,756.7
1,000cc	1,200cc	155.1	167.7	176.8	175.3	153.7	173.0	167.7	171.2	184.2	2,258.2
1,200cc	1,500cc	389.4	469.5	508.6	463.0	366.3	379.8	380.3	379.9	342.8	5,225.3
1,500cc	1,800cc	511.7	603.1	634.0	551.0	463.2	430.3	489.4	530.1	538.6	6,344.6
1,800cc	2,000cc	199.8	269.7	341.7	313.6	258.1	284.7	359.5	381.1	349.3	3,273.7
2,000cc	2,500cc	56.8	55.2	53.0	44.1	38.3	40.6	55.3	87.0	95.9	791.2
2,500cc	3,000cc	31.1	44.0	52.7	44.0	29.1	26.4	27.6	35.4	50.6	494.3
3,000cc		16.3	23.9	25.7	22.2	15.9	18.4	26.0	28.2	33.9	314.8
cc not known2		-	-	-	-	-	-	-	-	-	-
All capacities		1,541.6	1,843.7	1,974.0	1,750.3	1,416.7	1,410.0	1,571.4	1,682.9	1,660.9	20,504.9
Other vehicles		177.1	223.8	239.1	199.7	147.6	147.0	146.0	173.5	190.2	2,217.4
All PLG		1,718.7	2,067.6	2,213.1	1,950.0	1,564.3	1,557.0	1,717.4	1,856.3	1,851.0	22,722.2

(b) Motor cycles, scooters and mopeds: by engine size   Thousands

Over	Not over	1987	1988	1989	1990	1991	1992	1993	1994	1995	All years
	50cc	7.8	8.2	8.7	8.1	6.0	4.9	4.2	4.9	6.0	112.1
50cc	125cc	11.2	13.1	14.4	14.3	10.7	9.1	7.9	8.1	9.6	169.7
125cc	150cc	-	-	-	-	-	-	-	-	-	0.9
150cc	200cc	0.1	0.4	0.5	0.6	0.4	0.3	0.2	0.4	0.5	14.2
200cc	250cc	1.0	1.5	2.3	2.8	2.1	2.2	2.1	2.2	3.3	45.8
250cc	350cc	0.8	0.9	0.9	0.9	0.9	1.0	0.9	0.9	1.0	11.8
350cc	500cc	1.1	1.3	1.6	2.0	2.4	2.6	2.7	4.3	5.7	43.1
500cc		6.3	9.4	12.8	15.3	16.3	16.2	17.8	21.9	31.5	196.4
All over 50cc		20.6	26.6	32.5	36.0	32.8	31.3	31.6	37.7	51.7	481.9
All engine sizes		28.4	34.8	41.2	44.1	38.9	36.3	35.8	42.6	57.8	594.0

(c) Public transport vehicles: by seating capacity   Thousands

Over	Not over	1987	1988	1989	1990	1991	1992	1993	1994	1995	All years
	4 seats	0.3	-	-	-	-	-	-	-	-	2.6
4 seats	8 seats	0.2	0.6	0.6	0.6	0.5	0.5	0.4	0.5	1.0	5.5
All 8 seats or less		0.5	0.7	0.7	0.7	0.5	0.5	0.4	0.6	1.0	8.0
8 seats	32 seats	2.8	2.7	2.4	2.1	1.7	1.3	1.6	2.0	2.1	23.5
32 seats	48 seats	0.1	0.2	0.2	0.4	0.3	0.7	0.8	1.2	1.4	8.6
48 seats		1.1	1.9	2.3	1.7	1.0	0.9	1.1	0.9	1.7	41.6
All over 8 seats		4.0	4.8	4.9	4.2	3.0	2.9	3.5	4.2	5.2	73.8
All capacities		4.5	5.5	5.6	4.9	3.5	3.5	3.9	4.7	6.2	81.8

(d) General goods: by gross weight   Thousands

Over	Not over	1987	1988	1989	1990	1991	1992	1993	1994	1995	All years
3.5 tonnes	7.5 tonnes	10.9	15.0	16.4	13.4	9.7	9.6	10.0	12.4	13.9	143.8
7.5 tonnes	12 tonnes	1.1	1.4	1.7	1.5	1.0	1.1	1.3	1.0	1.2	15.3
12 tonnes	25 tonnes	9.8	13.8	15.1	11.6	7.5	7.1	7.6	8.5	9.8	117.6
25 tonnes	33 tonnes	3.4	5.2	6.1	3.7	2.8	2.9	4.8	7.7	8.2	52.3
33 tonnes	38 tonnes	4.6	7.5	8.9	5.9	4.4	5.4	7.6	10.2	13.2	76.4
38 tonnes		-	-	-	-	-	-	-	0.1	0.5	0.7
Gross weight unknowr		-	-	-	-	-	-	-	-	-	-
All vehicles		29.9	43.0	48.3	36.1	25.4	26.1	31.2	40.0	46.8	406.3

Table 4 (continued)

(e) Farmers' goods: by gross weight/Abolished - vehicles will move to other groups on renewal of tax disk.   Thousands

Over	Not over	Pre 1979	1979	1980	1981	1982	1983	1984	1985	1986
	3.5 tonnes	0.5	0.2	0.3	0.3	0.2	0.3	0.5	0.7	0.7
3.5 tonnes	7.5 tonnes	0.3	-	-	0.1	0.1	0.2	0.2	0.3	0.2
7.5 tonnes	12 tonnes	-	-	-	-	-	-	-	-	-
12 tonnes	25 tonnes	-	-	-	-	0.1	0.1	0.1	0.2	0.2
25 tonnes	33 tonnes	-	-	-	-	-	-	-	-	-
33 tonnes	38 tonnes	-	-	-	-	-	-	-	-	-
38 tonnes										
Gross weight unknown		0.8	-	-	-	0.2	0.2	0.2	0.2	0.1
All vehicles		1.8	0.4	0.5	0.5	0.7	0.9	1.1	1.4	1.2

(f) Special machines/Special concession group (Mainly agricultural tractors and machinery)   Thousands

	Pre 1979	1979	1980	1981	1982	1983	1984	1985	1986
Agricultural tractors	39.6	5.9	4.8	5.5	7.3	8.6	9.1	9.7	7.2
Combine harvesters and other agricultural machinery	6.0	0.7	0.6	0.7	1.0	1.3	1.6	1.8	1.6
Mowing machines	-	-	-	-	-	-	-	0.1	0.2
Electric	7.5	0.7	0.7	0.7	0.6	0.5	0.4	0.5	0.5
Gritting vehicle	-	-	-	-	-	0.1	0.2	0.2	0.2
Snow plough	0.1	-	-	-	-	-	-	-	-
Steam vehicles	-	-	-	-	-	-	-	-	-
All vehicles	53.3	7.3	6.3	7.0	9.0	10.7	11.4	12.2	9.7

(g) Other licensed vehicles   Thousands

	Pre 1979	1979	1980	1981	1982	1983	1984	1985	1986
Three wheelers less than 450 kgs	5.2	1.5	1.6	1.3	2.2	2.2	2.2	1.9	1.8
General haulage	-	-	-	-	-	-	-	-	0.1
Recovery	1.5	0.4	0.6	0.6	0.8	0.9	1.0	1.0	0.9
All vehicles	6.8	2.0	2.2	1.9	3.0	3.1	3.2	3.0	2.8

(h) Crown and other vehicles exempt from licence duty   Thousands

	Pre 1979	1979	1980	1981	1982	1983	1984	1985	1986
Crown vehicles	5.2	0.4	0.4	0.5	0.5	0.5	0.6	0.5	0.7
Other exempt:									
Disabled	9.4	4.0	5.5	9.0	17.4	27.8	32.6	37.8	38.6
Over 25 years old	102.9	0.5	0.6	0.6	0.6	0.8	0.9	0.5	0.5
Others	184.2	3.8	4.2	4.1	4.6	9.8	13.1	5.3	4.8
All other exempt	296.5	8.4	10.4	13.7	22.6	38.3	46.6	43.7	43.9
All exempt vehicles	301.7	8.8	10.7	14.2	23.1	38.8	47.2	44.2	44.6

(i) Special vehicles group: Tax classes 14 and 15   Thousands

	Pre 1979	1979	1980	1981	1982	1983	1984	1985	1986
Special vehicles group	2.2	0.6	0.4	0.4	0.6	0.7	1.0	0.9	1.1

(j) Other abolished tax groups/Vehicles will transfer to other tax groups on renewal of tax disk.   Thousands

	Pre 1979	1979	1980	1981	1982	1983	1984	1985	1986
Digging machines	1.3	0.3	0.3	0.2	0.3	0.4	0.5	0.5	0.6
Mobile cranes	0.7	0.1	0.1	-	-	-	0.1	0.1	0.1
Works trucks	0.5	0.1	0.2	0.2	0.2	0.3	0.3	0.4	0.5

1 The vehicle taxation system was subject to major revisions in 1995: See supplement.
2 Counts of vehicles in 'Private and light goods' have been estimated up to 1991.
3 Until end June 1995 also included showman's haulage.

Table 4 (continued)

(e) Farmers' goods: by gross weight/Abolished - vehicles will move to other groups on renewal of tax disk.   Thousands

Over	Not over	1987	1988	1989	1990	1991	1992	1993	1994	1995	All years
	3.5 tonnes	0.6	0.7	0.7	0.6	0.4	0.3	0.2	0.2	0.1	7.5
3.5 tonnes	7.5 tonnes	0.2	0.2	0.2	-	-	-	-	-	-	2.3
7.5 tonnes	12 tonnes	-	-	-	-	-	-	-	-	-	0.4
12 tonnes	25 tonnes	0.1	0.2	0.1	-	-	-	-	-	-	1.7
25 tonnes	33 tonnes	-	-	-	-	-	-	-	-	-	0.4
33 tonnes	38 tonnes	-	-	-	-	-	-	-	-	-	0.2
38 tonnes											
Gross weight unknown		0.1	0.1	0.1	-	-	-	-	-	-	2.3
All vehicles		1.1	1.3	1.2	0.9	0.5	0.3	0.3	0.3	0.2	14.7

(f) Special machines/Special concession group (Mainly agricultural tractors and machinery)   Thousands

	1987	1988	1989	1990	1991	1992	1993	1994	1995	All years
Agricultural tractors	8.1	10.8	10.6	10.3	9.5	9.6	13.6	14.7	18.5	203.4
Combine harvesters and other agricultural machinery	1.8	2.2	2.5	2.4	2.4	2.6	3.6	4.4	6.8	44.0
Mowing machines	0.2	0.4	0.5	0.7	0.6	0.8	0.8	0.9	0.9	6.5
Electric	0.5	0.5	0.5	0.5	0.5	0.4	0.4	0.4	0.4	16.3
Gritting vehicle	0.3	0.3	0.2	0.2	0.2	0.1	0.2	0.1	0.2	2.6
Snow plough	-	-	-	-	0.2	0.1	0.1	-	-	1.2
Steam vehicles	-	-	-	-	-	-	-	-	-	-
All vehicles	10.9	14.3	14.4	14.2	13.3	13.8	18.7	20.6	26.8	274.0

(g) Other licensed vehicles   Thousands

	1987	1988	1989	1990	1991	1992	1993	1994	1995	All years
Three wheelers less than 450 kgs	1.7	1.7	1.2	1.0	0.1	1.0	0.8	0.7	0.6	28.7
General haulage	0.1	0.2	0.2	0.1	-	-	-	-	0.1	1.6
Recovery	0.9	2.1	0.8	0.6	0.4	0.2	0.2	0.3	0.3	13.3
All vehicles	2.7	3.9	2.3	1.7	0.6	1.3	1.1	1.1	1.0	43.6

(h) Crown and other vehicles exempt from licence duty   Thousands

	1987	1988	1989	1990	1991	1992	1993	1994	1995	All years
Crown vehicles	0.7	0.6	1.0	1.1	1.0	1.6	1.4	1.6	1.3	19.5
Other exempt:										
Disabled	41.3	47.8	49.0	41.8	32.6	33.9	81.9	97.9	109.7	718.1
Over 25 years old	0.7	1.0	1.4	1.7	1.5	1.3	1.2	1.2	2.1	120.0
Others	5.0	5.8	6.9	6.9	7.2	8.5	10.1	11.8	15.5	311.6
All other exempt	46.9	54.6	57.3	50.3	41.3	43.8	93.2	110.9	127.3	1,149.7
All exempt vehicles	47.6	55.3	58.3	51.4	42.3	45.4	94.5	112.5	128.6	1,169.2

(i) Special vehicles group: Tax classes 14 and 15   Thousands

	1987	1988	1989	1990	1991	1992	1993	1994	1995	All years
Special vehicles group	1.4	2.3	2.3	1.9	1.5	1.3	2.0	3.0	4.1	27.6

(j) Other abolished tax groups/Vehicles will transfer to other tax groups on renewal   Thousands

	1987	1988	1989	1990	1991	1992	1993	1994	1995	All years
Digging machines	0.8	1.3	1.6	1.2	1.0	0.9	1.2	1.9	2.7	17.0
Mobile cranes	-	0.2	0.3	0.2	-	-	-	-	0.2	3.0
Works trucks	0.7	1.2	1.6	0.8	0.6	0.6	0.8	1.8	2.3	13.1

1 The vehicle taxation system was subject to major revisions in 1995: See supplement.
2 Counts of vehicles in 'Private and light goods' have been estimated up to 1991.
3 Until end June 1995 also included showman's haulage.

Table 5 Motor vehicles currently licensed 1995: by propulsion type [1]

					Thousands
Taxation class:	Petrol	Diesel	Electric	Others[2]	All
Private and light goods	19,625.1	3,093.5	-	3.6	22,722.2
of which: body type cars	18,674.5	1,827.5	-	2.9	20,504.9
Motor cycles scooters and mopeds	593.4	0.6	-	-	594.0
Bus	1.5	48.7	-	-	50.1
Abolished: Hackney	1.1	30.5	-	-	31.6
Goods	2.7	400.9	-	-	403.7
Abolished: Showman's & Farmers goods	-	7.6	-	-	7.7
Abolished: Farmers light goods	3.7	6.1	-	-	9.8
Special concessionary group	7.0	250.1	16.3	0.6	274.0
Special vehicles group	0.4	26.2	-	0.9	27.6
Other vehicles	29.8	13.8	-	-	43.6
Abolished: Other	1.0	34.2	-	0.6	35.9
Exempt vehicles	1,002.6	161.3	3.9	1.5	1,169.2
All vehicles	21,268.6	4,073.3	20.3	7.3	25,369.4
of which:					
Body type cars: All	19,499.8	1,891.3	-	3.0	21,394.2
Body type cars: Company	1,674.2	555.7	-	0.8	2,230.7

1 The vehicle taxation system was subject to major revisions in 1995: See supplement
2 Includes steam powered, gas and petrol/gas.

Table 6 Motorcars[1] currently licensed:
Original registrations [2] and licensing rates: 1995

Year of first registration	Original registrations (thousands)	Currently licensed (thousands)	Licensing rate percentage
1995	1,927	1,778	92.2
1994	1,896	1,787	94.2
1993	1,769	1,658	93.7
1992	1,592	1,448	90.9
1991	1,592	1,452	91.2
1990	1,996	1,793	89.9
1989	2,294	2,024	88.2
1988	2,201	1,892	85.9
1987	1,923	1,582	82.3
1986	1,767	1,362	77.1
1985	1,807	1,258	69.6
1984	1,753	1,039	59.2
1983	1,746	825	47.2
1982	1,535	520	33.9
1981	1,448	284	19.6
1980	1,439	171	11.9
1979	1,588	118	7.5
Pre 1979	10,008	404	4.0
All	40,282	21,394	53.1

1 Vehicles with car body types in all taxation classes.
  For similar information for 1988, 1991, 1994 see VLS 1994 edition,
  for similar information for 1987, 1990, 1993 see VLS 1993 edition,
  for 1986, 1989, 1992 see VLS 1992 edition.
2 Vehicles registered at DVLA and remaining on file.
  This excludes vehicles subject to direct or personal export,
  but retains scrapped vehicles.

Table 7 Motorcars currently licensed 1995: By year of first registration

Vehicles with car body types in all taxation classes: by cylinder capacity

Petrol propulsion   Thousands

Over	Not over	Pre 1979	1979	1980	1981	1982	1983	1984	1985	1986
	700cc	3.2	0.8	0.8	1.5	2.5	2.7	3.0	4.2	5.7
700cc	1,000cc	59.2	16.6	23.8	56.0	69.5	106.0	129.3	145.8	160.0
1,000cc	1,200cc	61.5	21.4	29.2	42.3	77.3	106.2	140.4	151.2	151.3
1,200cc	1,500cc	94.9	28.0	50.4	81.9	149.1	233.8	290.4	334.2	355.3
1,500cc	1,800cc	68.1	18.2	27.7	47.9	122.8	219.1	282.2	378.5	417.3
1,800cc	2,000cc	27.2	11.0	14.1	19.9	41.8	73.8	88.8	116.1	130.5
2,000cc	2,500cc	24.0	9.6	11.4	17.2	26.6	36.5	39.8	41.9	48.0
2,500cc	3,000cc	23.1	6.1	6.4	7.9	15.8	24.1	25.0	27.5	27.4
3,000cc		38.2	5.5	6.1	6.7	8.3	10.9	13.1	15.3	14.0
not known/ not applicable		0.5	-	-	-	-	-	-	-	-
All capacities		399.9	117.3	169.8	281.2	513.7	813.2	1,012.2	1,214.8	1,309.6

Diesel propulsion

Over	Not over	Pre 1979	1979	1980	1981	1982	1983	1984	1985	1986
	700cc	-	-	-	-	-	-	-	-	-
700cc	1,000cc	-	-	-	-	-	-	0.4	0.6	0.3
1,000cc	1,200cc	-	-	-	-	-	-	-	-	-
1,200cc	1,500cc	-	0.2	0.2	-	-	-	-	0.1	0.1
1,500cc	1,800cc	-	-	0.1	1.5	3.5	4.6	14.2	27.2	35.1
1,800cc	2,000cc	0.2	-	-	0.1	-	1.3	3.5	5.6	7.4
2,000cc	2,500cc	1.7	0.5	0.7	0.9	1.5	4.4	6.7	7.1	7.5
2,500cc	3,000cc	0.3	-	-	0.1	0.4	0.7	0.7	1.4	1.6
3,000cc		1.1	0.3	0.3	0.5	0.7	0.6	0.6	0.6	0.6
not known/ not applicable		-	-	-	-	-	-	-	-	-
All capacities		3.7	1.1	1.5	3.2	6.4	11.8	26.3	42.7	52.8

All propulsion types (includes electricity, steam, gas and petrol/gas)

Over	Not over	Pre 1979	1979	1980	1981	1982	1983	1984	1985	1986
	700cc	3.3	0.8	0.8	1.5	2.5	2.7	3.1	4.2	5.8
700cc	1,000cc	59.2	16.6	23.8	56.0	69.5	106.0	129.7	146.4	160.3
1,000cc	1,200cc	61.5	21.4	29.2	42.3	77.3	106.3	140.5	151.3	151.3
1,200cc	1,500cc	95.0	28.2	50.6	82.0	149.2	233.9	290.5	334.4	355.4
1,500cc	1,800cc	68.2	18.3	27.8	49.4	126.3	223.8	296.5	405.7	452.4
1,800cc	2,000cc	27.4	11.1	14.2	20.0	41.9	75.1	92.3	121.7	137.9
2,000cc	2,500cc	25.7	10.1	12.1	18.0	28.2	40.9	46.6	49.0	55.5
2,500cc	3,000cc	23.5	6.1	6.5	8.1	16.3	24.8	25.7	28.9	29.0
3,000cc		39.3	5.8	6.4	7.2	9.0	11.5	13.7	15.9	14.6
not known/ not applicable		0.6	-	-	-	-	-	-	0.1	-
All capacities		403.6	118.4	171.4	284.5	520.2	825.0	1,038.6	1,257.6	1,362.4

Table 7 (continued)

Vehicles with car body types in all taxation classes: by cylinder capacity

Thousands

Over	Not over	1987	1988	1989	1990	1991	1992	1993	1994	1995	All
	700cc	6.3	5.3	3.9	1.8	0.9	0.9	1.3	1.7	1.3	47.8
700cc	1,000cc	178.9	209.9	181.6	138.4	93.7	57.2	68.5	73.9	69.2	1,837.5
1,000cc	1,200cc	158.5	171.3	180.8	179.0	157.2	178.2	183.6	186.6	206.0	2,382.0
1,200cc	1,500cc	399.7	481.6	519.4	471.1	372.7	385.2	392.8	403.9	389.2	5,433.9
1,500cc	1,800cc	485.9	576.7	598.4	512.9	413.3	358.8	388.6	394.7	401.6	5,712.8
1,800cc	2,000cc	188.4	255.0	317.7	285.1	224.4	227.4	240.1	232.6	220.9	2,714.8
2,000cc	2,500cc	47.3	42.3	40.7	32.2	24.7	23.7	29.4	48.7	51.3	595.2
2,500cc	3,000cc	30.5	42.0	50.2	40.7	25.2	23.2	23.1	25.0	37.1	460.3
3,000cc		16.2	23.9	25.5	22.3	15.9	16.3	21.8	24.2	30.4	314.5
not known/ not applicable		-	-	-	-	-	-	-	-	-	1.1
All capacities		1,511.7	1,808.1	1,918.3	1,683.4	1,328.0	1,271.0	1,349.2	1,391.3	1,407.1	19,499.8

Diesel propulsion Thousands

Over	Not over	1987	1988	1989	1990	1991	1992	1993	1994	1995	All
	700cc	-	-	-	-	-	-	0.1	0.2	0.2	1.2
700cc	1,000cc	0.3	0.4	0.2	0.2	0.2	0.3	0.2	0.1	0.1	3.5
1,000cc	1,200cc	-	0.1	0.2	0.1	0.2	0.2	0.2	0.3	0.2	2.0
1,200cc	1,500cc	-	0.3	2.9	4.6	3.9	7.1	30.1	31.0	9.4	90.3
1,500cc	1,800cc	40.0	42.3	51.6	51.8	60.7	82.2	115.6	152.9	161.4	844.9
1,800cc	2,000cc	17.2	22.2	32.5	35.6	39.1	62.7	125.7	155.4	133.6	642.3
2,000cc	2,500cc	11.1	14.3	13.5	12.7	14.2	17.5	26.6	39.3	46.3	226.4
2,500cc	3,000cc	1.4	3.1	3.6	4.2	4.5	3.8	5.1	11.0	14.4	56.7
3,000cc		0.5	0.7	0.9	0.7	0.6	2.7	4.7	4.0	3.6	23.8
not known/ not applicable		-	-	-	-	-	-	-	-	-	0.2
All capacities		70.6	83.4	105.4	110.1	123.5	176.5	308.5	394.2	369.3	1,891.3

All propulsion types (includes electricity, steam, gas and petrol/gas) Thousands

Over	Not over	1987	1988	1989	1990	1991	1992	1993	1994	1995	All
	700cc	6.3	5.3	4.0	1.8	0.9	1.0	1.5	1.9	1.5	49.0
700cc	1,000cc	179.2	210.2	181.8	138.6	93.9	57.6	68.7	74.0	69.4	1,841.0
1,000cc	1,200cc	158.5	171.5	181.0	179.1	157.3	178.4	183.8	186.9	206.2	2,384.0
1,200cc	1,500cc	399.8	481.8	522.3	475.8	376.6	392.4	422.9	434.9	399.0	5,524.8
1,500cc	1,800cc	525.9	619.1	650.1	564.6	474.0	440.9	504.3	547.7	563.1	6,558.1
1,800cc	2,000cc	205.6	277.2	350.2	320.7	263.5	290.1	365.8	388.0	354.6	3,357.2
2,000cc	2,500cc	58.4	56.6	54.1	44.9	38.9	41.2	56.0	88.0	97.6	821.7
2,500cc	3,000cc	31.9	45.1	53.8	44.9	29.7	27.1	28.3	36.3	51.6	517.4
3,000cc		16.7	24.6	26.4	23.0	16.5	18.9	26.5	28.8	34.8	339.6
not known/ not applicable		-	-	-	-	-	-	-	-	-	1.4
All capacities		1,582.4	1,891.5	2,023.7	1,793.5	1,451.6	1,447.6	1,657.8	1,786.6	1,777.9	21,394.2

Table 8 Motor vehicles currently licensed: by taxation group: region: 1995

Thousands

County region country	Private and light goods		Motor cycles scooters and mopeds	Public transport vehicles[1]	Goods[2]	Special concession	Other vehicles	Crown and other exempt vehicles	All vehicles	of which: body type cars	
	Body type cars	Other vehicles								All	Per cent company
Cleveland	168.2	15.9	3.8	0.6	3.0	2.0	3.6	11.4	208.5	180.1	4.2
Cumbria	178.1	20.8	5.8	0.6	4.6	7.0	8.2	7.0	232.0	186.4	9.1
Durham	170.3	17.7	3.6	1.2	3.9	2.8	4.2	15.2	218.8	185.9	4.5
Northumberland	90.3	8.8	2.1	0.2	1.7	3.6	2.3	4.4	113.4	94.9	4.1
Tyne and Wear	281.6	26.6	4.2	2.0	5.2	1.4	5.2	21.3	347.5	303.7	8.8
Northern	888.4	89.9	19.5	4.6	18.4	16.9	23.4	59.3	1120.2	951.1	6.7
Humberside	268.8	28.2	14.2	0.9	6.3	6.7	8.0	10.3	343.4	280.6	6.6
North Yorkshire	263.2	32.3	10.9	0.8	8.0	12.5	9.6	6.1	343.3	271.0	7.3
South Yorkshire	407.0	45.4	10.1	2.2	10.1	3.4	9.3	28.7	516.1	437.4	7.0
West Yorkshire	653.0	67.6	13.9	2.6	16.9	5.6	13.9	29.6	803.0	685.4	11.5
Yorks & H'side	1591.9	173.6	49.1	6.4	41.3	28.2	40.7	74.7	2005.9	1674.4	8.8
Derbyshire	276.7	35.1	9.3	1.5	6.5	4.6	8.8	9.9	352.4	288.5	11.4
Leicestershire	326.3	32.5	9.7	1.1	6.0	3.8	9.1	8.2	396.6	337.0	12.2
Lincolnshire	228.4	26.8	9.3	0.9	5.8	14.2	9.8	7.4	302.6	238.0	6.5
Northamptonshire	220.2	22.0	6.7	0.8	7.0	2.5	5.7	6.6	271.4	227.3	12.1
Nottinghamshire	353.5	36.3	11.6	1.0	8.1	3.8	9.1	18.0	441.4	373.3	7.6
East Midlands	1405.1	152.5	46.6	5.2	33.4	28.8	42.6	50.2	1764.5	1464.1	9.9
Cambridgeshire	283.1	33.2	10.8	0.8	6.8	8.2	8.8	6.4	358.1	291.5	11.1
Norfolk	308.2	36.6	14.5	1.0	5.9	10.5	12.1	7.4	396.2	318.4	8.7
Suffolk	260.9	28.8	12.5	0.6	7.3	6.9	8.8	7.1	332.9	270.0	6.0
East Anglia	852.2	98.6	37.7	2.5	20.0	25.6	29.7	20.8	1087.2	879.8	8.7
Bedfordshire	210.5	21.7	5.6	0.9	3.5	2.0	5.7	4.1	253.9	216.3	9.9
Berkshire	383.4	36.5	8.8	0.8	6.2	1.9	7.7	4.7	450.1	390.7	21.4
Buckinghamshire	286.5	23.9	6.7	0.4	7.2	2.2	6.1	4.2	337.2	293.0	16.8
East Sussex	255.2	26.1	7.6	1.3	2.7	1.9	7.0	6.3	308.0	264.2	4.8
Essex	612.6	66.0	19.0	1.9	9.9	6.1	17.0	14.4	746.9	633.0	5.8
Greater London	2263.5	220.4	62.1	7.9	32.8	2.5	46.3	48.7	2684.2	2325.6	14.9
Hampshire	632.4	60.4	23.3	1.2	7.8	7.2	17.1	13.0	762.4	650.8	7.1
Hertfordshire	519.7	52.3	13.6	0.8	8.5	3.2	10.9	7.3	616.3	530.6	16.9
Isle of Wight	46.0	5.6	2.5	0.2	0.4	0.6	1.8	1.3	58.5	48.1	2.6
Kent	589.8	60.3	20.7	1.8	9.2	5.5	17.6	13.9	718.8	608.6	6.1
Oxfordshire	232.3	23.7	9.1	0.7	3.9	3.7	7.3	3.2	284.0	238.2	8.5
Surrey	451.6	43.5	12.9	1.1	6.3	1.8	12.1	5.0	534.2	461.5	8.3
West Sussex	310.3	32.2	8.5	0.2	3.0	2.3	7.3	5.2	369.0	318.3	9.5
South East	6793.9	672.7	200.3	19.1	101.5	40.7	164.0	131.3	8123.5	6978.7	11.7
Avon	370.2	39.2	14.3	1.4	8.1	2.8	10.2	8.2	454.4	381.8	8.5
Cornwall	177.0	23.3	8.5	0.8	2.7	5.9	8.0	6.8	233.0	185.9	3.8
Devonshire	386.2	48.8	17.2	1.7	5.5	10.4	13.8	11.6	495.3	402.1	4.8
Dorset	277.0	29.3	10.9	0.9	2.9	3.9	9.3	6.0	340.1	286.6	4.5
Gloucestershire	228.3	24.3	9.5	0.7	3.2	3.6	8.0	4.9	282.5	235.8	6.5
Somerset	188.2	23.2	7.6	0.5	7.0	6.0	8.1	3.9	244.5	194.6	5.0
Wiltshire	303.1	30.2	9.9	0.5	5.7	4.8	7.7	5.3	367.3	310.6	26.6
South West	1930.1	218.3	77.9	6.5	35.0	37.3	65.2	46.8	2417.2	1997.4	9.0

Table 8 Motor vehicles currently licensed: by taxation group: region: 1995

Thousands

County region country	Private and light goods		Motor cycles scooters and mopeds	Public transport vehicles[1]	Goods[2]	Special concession	All other vehicles	Crown and other exempt vehicles	All vehicles	of which: body type cars	
	Body type cars	Other vehicles								All	Per cent company
Hereford & Worcs	287.0	33.4	9.6	0.9	5.6	6.6	10.4	6.6	360.1	297.0	13.0
Salop	166.8	20.7	5.0	0.4	4.3	7.3	5.9	5.5	215.9	173.9	8.2
Staffordshire	357.9	37.0	12.0	1.6	8.8	4.3	9.5	17.0	448.1	377.0	7.2
Warwickshire	209.1	21.7	6.2	0.6	4.2	2.6	7.9	5.0	257.3	215.8	21.2
West Midlands	1038.5	157.7	19.1	3.1	28.5	4.2	18.8	38.7	1308.7	1081.9	19.6
West Midlands	2059.3	270.4	52.0	6.6	51.4	25.1	52.5	72.9	2590.2	2145.5	15.7
Cheshire	362.0	36.8	11.2	0.9	8.8	4.4	8.3	16.6	449.1	381.0	6.7
Gtr Manchester	858.9	100.4	14.6	2.5	25.6	2.9	14.0	40.8	1059.7	902.5	19.3
Lancashire	516.4	54.0	14.3	2.8	12.4	5.7	11.5	28.7	645.7	547.0	6.0
Merseyside	367.4	34.5	7.7	2.4	6.7	1.1	6.4	40.8	466.9	408.9	5.9
North Western	2104.7	225.7	47.8	8.6	53.5	14.1	40.2	126.9	2621.5	2239.4	11.5
England	17625.6	1901.7	530.9	59.4	354.5	216.7	458.3	583.0	21730.1	18330.3	11.0
Clwyd	144.4	16.2	4.0	0.4	3.2	2.7	4.3	9.6	184.8	155.0	5.0
Dyfed	121.9	18.4	3.0	0.7	3.3	5.5	6.2	8.5	167.5	131.3	3.2
Gwent	148.0	16.1	3.8	0.9	3.1	1.6	3.4	13.1	189.8	161.7	4.9
Gwynedd	82.1	12.0	2.1	0.7	1.7	2.6	2.7	4.5	108.3	87.1	3.1
Mid Glamorgan	139.1	13.9	2.8	0.8	2.6	0.7	2.5	18.9	181.3	158.5	3.9
Powys	42.6	8.5	1.0	0.2	1.7	3.7	2.5	1.4	61.7	44.4	5.1
South Glamorgan	116.7	9.8	1.6	0.5	2.1	0.5	1.8	5.1	137.9	122.1	21.8
West Glamorgan	113.4	10.7	2.5	0.8	1.4	0.5	2.2	11.8	143.4	125.4	4.9
Wales	908.3	105.6	20.7	4.8	19.1	17.8	25.7	72.9	1174.8	985.5	6.5
Borders	38.0	5.1	0.6	0.2	0.8	2.4	1.2	1.0	49.2	39.1	7.3
Central Scotland	92.5	8.8	1.3	0.4	2.6	1.1	1.5	5.0	113.3	97.7	15.1
Dumfries & Galloway	50.9	6.5	1.3	0.1	1.9	3.9	1.8	2.0	68.5	53.1	5.9
Fife	107.7	9.4	2.0	0.6	1.6	2.0	2.0	6.1	131.3	114.1	4.2
Grampian	188.8	20.2	4.1	1.0	4.7	7.4	5.8	3.8	236.0	193.5	7.4
Highland	68.0	10.2	1.7	0.3	1.6	2.7	2.8	2.1	89.5	70.5	5.2
Lothian	243.6	23.4	3.8	1.3	3.8	2.3	5.4	13.5	297.2	254.9	14.8
Orkney	7.0	1.4	0.3	0.1	0.3	1.0	0.6	0.1	10.6	7.2	4.9
Shetland	8.0	2.0	0.3	0.1	0.3	0.3	0.4	0.1	11.5	8.1	6.0
Strathclyde	589.4	56.7	6.2	3.9	12.5	6.1	9.5	48.9	733.3	639.3	7.7
Tayside	128.8	13.2	2.1	0.5	2.8	5.0	3.4	4.7	160.7	134.1	6.9
Western Isles	6.4	1.4	0.1	0.1	0.2	0.3	0.3	0.2	9.0	6.6	4.1
Scotland	1529.1	158.4	23.8	8.6	33.1	34.5	34.8	87.6	1909.9	1618.4	8.7
County unknown	73.5	6.7	2.1	0.1	1.1	0.6	1.4	2.3	87.9	76.2	7.2
No current keeper vehicle under disposal	368.4	44.9	16.6	0.8	5.6	4.3	9.4	16.7	466.7	383.8	0.0
Great Britain	20504.9	2217.4	594.0	73.8	413.4	274.0	529.5	762.5	25369.4	21394.2	10.4

1 Tax class 34 (Bus) and abolished tax class 35 (Hackney) with more than 8 seats

2 Includes agricultural vans and lorries but excludes electrical goods vehicles.

31

Table 9 Motor vehicles currently licensed:[1] 1903-1984

For detail of years 1985-1995 see table 1

Thousands

| Year | Private and light goods[2] | | Goods vehicles[3,4] | M'cycles scooters and mopeds[5] | Public transport vehicles[6] | Special machines etc[7] | Other vehicles[8] | Crown and exempt vehicles[9] | All vehicles |
	Private cars	Other vehicles							
1903	8		4	..	5	..	..	..	17
1909	53		30	36	24	..	..	..	143
1920	187		101	228	75	..	..	..	591
1930	1056		349	712	101	15	15	24	2272
1939	2034		488	418	90	31	3	84	3148
1946	1770		560	449	105	146	16	61	3107
1950	1979	439	439	643	123	262	24	61	3970
1951	2095	457	451	725	123	250	26	63	4190
1952	2221	477	450	812	119	270	29	86	4464
1953	2446	516	446	889	105	289	30	88	4809
1954	2733	566	450	977	97	307	32	88	5250
1955	3109	633	462	1076	92	326	35	89	5822
1956	3437	685	471	1137	89	336	37	95	6287
1957	3707	723	473	1261	87	355	41	96	6743
1958	4047	772	461	1300	86	367	46	96	7175
1959	4416	824	473	1479	83	383	55	96	7809
1960	4900	894	493	1583	84	392	65	101	8512
1961	5296	944	508	1577	82	400	76	106	8989
1962	5776	1002	512	1567	84	401	83	107	9532
1963	6462	1092	535	1546	86	412	88	115	10336
1964	7190	1184	551	1534	86	421	90	120	11176
1965	7732	1240	584	1420	86	417	91	127	11697
1966	8210	1283	577	1239	85	399	87	142	12022
1967	8882	1358	593	1190	85	416	89	147	12760
1968	9285	1388	580	1082	89	409	92	157	13082
1969	9672	1408	547	993	92	398	90	162	13362
1970	9971	1421	545	923	93	385	89	121	13548
1971	10443	1452	542	899	96	380	92	126	14030
1972	11006	1498	525	866	95	371	95	128	14584
1973	11738	1559	540	887	96	373	97	137	15427
1974	11917	1547	539	918	96	380	96	149	15642
1975	12526	1592	553	1077	105	384	108	166	16511
1976	13184	1626	563	1175	110	387	117	156	17318
1977	13220	1591	559	1190	110	393	115	167	17345
1978	13626	1597	549	1194	110	394	111	177	17758
1979	14162	1623	561	1292	111	402	106	359	18616
1980	14660	1641	507	1372	110	397	100	412	19199
1981	14867	1623	489	1371	110	365	95	427	19347
1982	15264	1624	477	1370	111	371	91	454	19762
1983	15543	1692	488	1290	113	376	86	621	20209
1984	16055	1752	490	1225	116	375	82	670	20765

1 The annual vehicle census of licensed vehicles has been taken as follows: 1903-1910 at 31 December; 1911-1920 at 31 March; 1921-1925 for the highest quarter; 1926-1938 for the September quarter; 1939-1945 at 31 August; 1946-1976 for the September quarter; 1977 census results are estimates; 1978 onward at 31 December.

2 From 1950 onwards, retrospective counts within the October 1982 taxation classes have been estimated. For years up to 1990, retrospective counts within these new taxation classes have been estimated. See Notes on taxation class changes.

3 Includes agricultural vans and lorries, showmens' goods vehicles licensed to draw trailers (note 2 applies).

4 Excludes electric goods vehicles which are now exempt from licence duty.

5 Includes scooters and mopeds.

6 Includes taxis. Prior to 1969, tram cars were included.

7 Includes agricultural tractors, combine harvesters, mowing machines, digging machines, mobile cranes and works trucks.

8 Includes three-wheelers, showmens' haulage and recovery vehicles.

9 Includes electric vehicles which during this period were exempt from licence duty and personal and direct export vehicles.

Table 10 Motor vehicles registered for the first time: by taxation group: 1985-95[1]

Thousands

	Private and light goods[2]			Public transportation vehicles				
Year	Body type cars	Other vehicles	Motor cycles scooters and mopeds	Hackney taxation class[3]	Bus taxation class[4]	Goods[6]	Special machines[7]	All other vehicles[9]
1985	1,804.0	225.5	125.8	6.8	3.7[5]	51.7	40.1	55.4
1986	1,839.3	231.4	106.4	8.9	5.5[5]	51.4	34.8	61.5
1987	1,962.7	249.9	90.8	8.7	5.0[5]	54.0	37.7	70.1
1988	2,154.7	282.3	90.1	9.2	5.0[5]	63.4	45.2	78.6
1989	2,241.2	294.0	97.3	8.0	5.1[5]	64.5	42.5	81.4
1990	1,942.3	237.6	94.4	7.4	4.5[5]	44.4	34.2	78.4
1991	1,536.6	171.9	76.5	5.2	3.0[5]	28.6	26.1	76.6
1992	1,528.0	166.4	65.6	5.1	3.1[5]	28.7	24.1	83.9
1993	1,694.6	158.8	58.4	5.4	3.6[5]	32.8	30.0	89.0
1994	1,809.1	182.6	64.6	6.7	4.2[5]	41.1	35.3	104.7
1995	1,828.3	195.7	68.9	..	5.2	48.0	33.3[8]	127.1

continued

			body type cars in all taxation classes					
					of which:			
Year	All vehicles	All body type cars	Company	Imported	Diesel	Per cent company	Per cent imports	Per cent diesel
1985	2,309.3	1,842.1	827.9	1,046.6	64.4	45	57	3
1986	2,333.7	1,883.2	867.7	1,018.0	74.9	46	54	4
1987	2,473.9	2,016.2	969.8	1,015.6	89.9	48	50	4
1988	2,723.5	2,210.3	1,131.4	1,216.0	99.2	51	55	4
1989	2,828.9	2,304.4	1,175.5	1,272.3	123.2	51	55	5
1990	2,438.7	2,005.1	1,049.9	1,117.5	125.4	52	56	6
1991	1,921.5	1,600.1	833.1	874.2	137.4	52	55	9
1992	1,901.8	1,599.1	826.7	874.5	195.8	52	55	12
1993	2,074.0	1,776.5	910.1	991.5	327.8	51	56	18
1994	2,249.0	1,906.4	996.4	1,082.1	418.8	52	57	22
1995	2,306.5	1,938.1	1,022.4	1,132.3	391.3	53	58	20

1 See supplement on recent taxation class changes, and also notes and definitions.
2 For years up to 1990 retrospective counts within these new taxation classes have been estimated.
3 Taxation class 35, Hackney. Public transportation vehicles including taxis: Abolished 30th June 1995
4 Taxation class 34, Buses. Public transportation vehicles with more than 8 seats. Introduced 1st July 1995.
5 Estimated: Retrospective estimates are based on vehicles registrations in tax class 35, with more than 8 seats
6 Until 30th June 1995 included agricultural vans and lorries and showman's goods vehicles licensed to draw trailers.
  From 1st July 1995 separate taxation groups for farmers and showmen were abolished.
7 The agricultural and special machines taxation group was abolished on 30th June 1995 and replaced by the
  special concession taxation group from 1st July 1995. See supplement.
8 The figure shown is aggregate number of vehicles registered in 1995 between 1st January and 30th June in agricultural
  and special machines group, and between 1st July and 31st December in special concession group.
9 Includes crown and exempt vehicles, three wheelers, and others. See supplement.

Table 11 Motor vehicles registered for the first time: by taxation group, vehicle details: 1985-1995

(a) Private and light goods: by engine size   Thousands

Over	Not over	1985	1986	1987	1988	1989	1990	1991	1992	1993	1994	1995
	1,000cc	225.5	236.3	245.5	260.5	222.0	162.0	104.3	64.7	73.4	78.6	76.5
1,000cc	1,200cc	217.3	205.9	198.2	195.8	196.2	183.0	153.4	176.3	180.8	184.1	203.8
1,200cc	1,500cc	507.6	508.1	520.7	576.6	600.5	531.0	406.2	412.3	415.5	415.2	387.4
1,500cc	1,800cc	669.0	689.8	723.4	782.5	799.6	681.0	557.2	521.7	576.2	623.7	650.3
1,800cc	2,000cc	220.4	234.1	312.7	387.5	462.2	403.0	321.6	344.4	405.3	427.2	399.3
2,000cc	2,500cc	95.4	104.7	111.8	108.5	109.7	102.0	104.4	115.1	135.1	184.6	206.8
2,500cc	3,000cc	44.4	43.3	45.8	57.4	66.5	56.0	38.2	34.5	33.8	43.6	60.5
3,000cc		26.9	24.6	26.2	34.6	37.2	32.7	23.2	25.3	33.3	34.5	39.4
cc not known		0.4	0.3	0.1	0.1	0.1	0.1	0.1	0.1	0.1	0.1	0.0
All vehicles		2,006.9	2,047.2	2,184.3	2,403.6	2,494.0	2151.7	1,708.5	1,694.2	1,853.4	1,991.6	2,024.0

Of which: Private and light goods: Diesel propulsion   Thousands

Over	Not over	1985	1986	1987	1988	1989	1990	1991	1992	1993	1994	1995
	1,000cc										0.6	0.8
1,000cc	1,200cc										0.4	0.3
1,200cc	1,500cc										29.4	9.4
1,500cc	1,800cc										210.9	217.8
1,800cc	2,000cc										174.9	157.4
2,000cc	2,500cc										130.0	149.3
2,500cc	3,000cc										15.7	20.7
3,000cc											6.0	5.5
cc not known											-	-
All vehicles											568.0	561.3

(b) Motor cycles, scooters and mopeds: by engine size   Thousands

Over	Not over	1985	1986	1987	1988	1989	1990	1991	1992	1993	1994	1995
	50cc	48.3	37.5	29.7	24.7	22.9	18.8	13.1	9.1	6.5	6.9	6.3
50cc	150cc	50.0	41.8	34.0	31.9	32.4	29.1	18.8	14.7	11.2	10.5	10.2
150cc	200cc	1.7	1.1	0.9	1.5	1.7	1.5	1.1	0.7	0.6	0.7	0.6
200cc	250cc	3.4	3.3	3.6	4.1	5.6	6.0	4.6	4.2	3.6	3.6	3.7
250cc	350cc	2.6	3.3	2.7	2.8	2.7	2.5	2.2	2.0	1.9	1.7	1.4
350cc	500cc	4.4	3.8	3.3	3.2	3.5	4.2	5.2	5.3	4.9	6.8	7.6
500cc		15.4	15.7	16.6	21.8	28.6	32.2	31.5	29.5	29.9	34.3	38.7
All vehicles		125.8	106.4	90.8	90.1	97.3	94.4	76.5	65.6	58.4	64.6	68.9

(c) Public transport vehicles: by seating capacity   Thousands

Over	Not over	1985	1986	1987	1988	1989	1990	1991	1992	1993	1994	1995
	4 seats	2.7	2.9	2.2	1.2	0.6	0.2	0.1	0.1	0.1	0.5	0.0
4 seats	8 seats	0.4	0.5	1.4	3.0	2.4	2.7	2.1	2.0	1.7	2.1	1.3
8 seats or less		3.1	3.4	3.6	4.2	3.0	2.9	2.2	2.0	1.8	2.5	1.3
8 seats	32 seats	1.3	3.5	3.6	2.7	2.3	2.2	1.6	1.4	1.7	1.9	2.1
32 seats	48 seats	0.3	0.2	0.2	0.2	0.3	0.5	0.3	0.6	0.8	1.2	1.4
48 seats		2.1	1.8	1.3	2.0	2.5	1.8	1.1	1.0	1.2	1.0	1.7
All over 8 seats		3.7	5.5	5.0	5.0	5.1	4.5	3.0	3.1	3.6	4.2	5.2
All capacities		6.8	8.9	8.7	9.2	8.2	7.7	5.2	5.1	5.4	6.7	

Table 11 (Continued) Motor vehicles registered for the first time: by taxation group, vehicle details: 1985-1995

(d) Goods: by gross weight   Thousands

Over	Not over	1988	1989	1990	1991	1992	1993	1994	1995
	3.5 tonnes	1.2	1.0	0.7	0.6	0.5	0.5	0.5	0.3
3.5 tonnes	7.5 tonnes	21.5	21.6	17.0	10.8	10.4	10.4	12.6	14.1
7.5 tonnes	12 tonnes	1.9	2.0	1.6	1.1	1.2	1.3	1.0	1.2
12 tonnes	25 tonnes	18.6	18.8	13.1	8.0	7.6	8.7	10.5	12.6
25 tonnes	33 tonnes	8.9	8.9	4.8	3.1	3.2	3.9	5.9	5.9
33 tonnes	38 tonnes	11.3	12.2	7.2	5.0	5.9	8.1	10.5	13.5
38 tonnes	40 tonnes	0.0	0.0	0.0	0.0	0.0	0.0	0.0	0.0
40 tonnes								0.1	0.5
Gross weight unknown		-	-	-	-	-	-	-	-
All vehicles		63.4	64.5	44.4	28.6	28.7	32.8	41.1	48.0

(e) Special machines, agricultural tractors etc.   Thousands

	1985	1986	1987	1988	1989	1990	1991	1992	1993	1994	1995
Agricultural tractors	24.3	18.6	19.6	21.8	19.3	17.6	14.6	13.9	17.7	18.3	19.0
Combine harvesters and other agricultural	3.7	2.6	2.7	3.0	3.0	2.8	2.4	2.5	2.5	2.5	3.3
Mowing machines	1.5	1.8	1.8	1.8	2.0	1.7	1.1	1.2	1.0	1.1	0.9
Electric											0.2
Gritting vehicle											0.1
Others	2.1	2.2	2.2	2.3	2.4	2.2	1.7	1.8	2.6	3.2	3.8
All vehicles	40.1	34.8	37.7	45.2	42.6	34.2	26.1	24.1	30.0	35.3	33.3

(f) Other licensed vehicles   Thousands

	1985	1986	1987	1988	1989	1990	1991	1992	1993	1994	1995
Tricycles	2.6	2.6	2.2	2.1	1.5	1.2	0.3	1.2	1.0	0.9	0.6
General haulage	0.4	0.4	0.4	0.4	0.2	0.1	0.1	0.1	0.1	..	0.0
Recovery vehicles	.	.	.	0.9	0.9	0.7	0.4	0.3	0.3	0.3	0.3
All vehicles	3.0	3.0	2.6	3.4	2.6	2.1	0.7	1.6	1.4	1.3	1.0

(g) Crown and other vehicles exempt from licence duty   Thousands

	1985	1986	1987	1988	1989	1990	1991	1992	1993	1994	1995
Crown vehicles	5.8	5.3	4.6	4.1	4.4	4.0	3.2	3.7	3.1	4.1	3.3
Personal and direct export vehicles	9.2	9.3	10.8	9.9	9.9	9.1	8.9	7.1	7.5	9.3	9.3
Other exempt vehicles	37.5	44.0	52.2	56.1	64.4	63.1	63.8	71.6	81.9	95.0	112.1
All exempt vehicles	52.5	58.5	67.5	70.1	78.6	76.2	75.8	82.3	92.4	108.4	121.4

(i) Special vehicles group: Tax classes 14 and 15

	1985	1986	1987	1988	1989	1990	1991	1992	1993	1994	1995
Special vehicles											3.3

(j) Other abolished tax groups (Jan - Jun 1995 only)   Thousands

	1985	1986	1987	1988	1989	1990	1991	1992	1993	1994	1995
Digging machines	4.6	5.1	6.1	8.5	7.5	5.5	3.7	2.9	3.9	5.8	3.2
Mobile cranes	0.5	0.5	0.4	0.9	0.9	0.8	0.3	0.2	0.2	0.3	0.2
Works trucks	3.5	4.0	4.9	7.0	7.4	3.7	2.3	1.7	2.1	4.1	2.5

Table 12 Motor vehicles registered for the first time: by county: 1995 with related stock and ownership information.

	1985	1995					
		All vehicles		Car in all taxation classes			
County region country	All vehicles currently licensed (thousands)	New registrations (thousands)	Currently licensed (thousands)	New registrations (thousands)	Currently licensed (thousands)	Per 1,000 population[1]	Average vehicle age (years)[2]
Cleveland	183	16.0	208.5	13.1	180.1	321	6.9
Cumbria	195	18.3	232.0	14.8	186.4	380	7.0
Durham	178	17.6	218.8	14.6	185.9	306	6.6
Northumberland	94	9.2	113.4	7.7	94.9	309	6.4
Tyne and Wear	290	37.9	347.5	32.6	303.7	268	6.4
Northern	940	98.9	1120.2	82.8	951.1	307	6.6
Humberside	305	25.1	343.4	19.7	280.6	315	6.9
North Yorkshire	292	27.8	343.3	20.9	271.0	373	6.6
South Yorkshire	411	38.8	516.1	30.3	437.4	335	7.0
West Yorkshire	667	72.2	803.0	59.8	685.4	326	6.3
Yorks & H'side	1,674	163.9	2005.9	130.8	1674.4	333	6.6
Derbyshire	289	45.3	352.4	36.3	288.5	302	7.0
Leicestershire	342	54.9	396.6	49.4	337.0	368	7.2
Lincolnshire	264	18.6	302.6	13.9	238.0	393	7.3
Northamptonshire	227	21.1	271.4	16.9	227.3	382	6.9
Nottinghamshire	380	29.5	441.4	23.9	373.3	362	7.3
East Midlands	1,501	169.3	1764.5	140.3	1464.1	357	7.1
Cambridgeshire	289	29.1	358.1	22.3	291.5	424	7.2
Norfolk	346	25.3	396.2	19.8	318.4	414	7.6
Suffolk	289	20.8	332.9	15.5	270.0	416	7.8
East Anglia	924	75.1	1087.2	57.6	879.8	418	7.5
Bedfordshire	238	20.3	253.9	16.9	216.3	398	7.2
Berkshire	363	61.3	450.1	54.3	390.7	508	6.5
Buckinghamshire	254	48.5	337.2	41.5	293.0	445	6.5
East Sussex	285	16.3	308.0	13.5	264.2	364	8.1
Essex	645	61.4	746.9	52.0	633.0	403	7.7
Greater London	2,583	314.0	2684.2	278.3	2325.6	334	7.4
Hampshire	673	53.0	762.4	43.6	650.8	405	7.7
Hertfordshire	510	75.1	616.3	66.2	530.6	528	6.7
Isle of Wight	54	2.6	58.5	2.2	48.1	385	9.0
Kent	643	45.0	718.8	36.5	608.6	394	7.7
Oxfordshire	251	23.9	284.0	20.2	238.2	404	7.4
Surrey	496	51.1	534.2	43.7	461.5	443	7.3
West Sussex	311	27.5	369.0	22.9	318.3	441	7.5
South East	7,307	800.0	8123.5	691.8	6978.7	391	7.4
Avon	419	11.3	454.4	9.8	381.8	390	7.8
Cornwall	207	10.9	233.0	8.5	185.9	388	8.4
Devonshire	435	26.4	495.3	20.6	402.1	382	8.2
Dorset	302	17.1	340.1	13.5	286.6	426	8.3
Gloucestershire	250	16.2	282.5	13.1	235.8	429	7.8
Somerset	215	11.5	244.5	8.3	194.6	407	8.3
Wiltshire	265	52.3	367.3	47.1	310.6	530	6.4
South West	2,092	145.8	2417.2	121	1997.4	416	7.9

1 Using mid year 1994 population estimates.

2 Nominal: Vehicles registered at any time in 1995 are counted as age 1 year at the end of 1995, vehicles registered in 1994 are counted as age 2 at the end of 1994, etc, etc.

Table 12 (cont'd.) Motor vehicles registered for the first time: by county: 1995 with related stock and ownership information.

County region country	1985 All vehicles currently licensed (thousands)	1995 All vehicles		1995 Car in all taxation classes			
		New registrations (thousands)	Currently licensed (thousands)	New registrations (thousands)	Currently licensed (thousands)	Per 1,000 population[1]	Average vehicle age (years)[2]
Hereford & Worcs	288	35.0	360.1	30.0	297.0	424	7.3
Salop	173	15.0	215.9	11.4	173.9	418	7.3
Staffordshire	376	32.3	448.1	25.4	377.0	358	7.2
Warwickshire	182	30.7	257.3	25.4	215.8	435	6.5
West Midlands	995	203.3	1308.7	173.6	1081.9	412	6.4
West Midlands	2,014	316.3	2590.2	265.9	2145.5	405	6.8
Cheshire	374	38.9	449.1	31.7	381.0	390	6.8
Gtr Manchester	824	131.1	1059.7	110.8	902.5	350	6.2
Lancashire	552	44.1	645.7	35.7	547.0	384	7.0
Merseyside	398	38.8	466.9	33.5	408.9	285	6.9
North Western	2,149	252.9	2621.5	211.7	2239.4	349	6.6
England	18,588	2022.3	21730.1	1701.9	18330.3	376	7.1
Clwyd	154	11.6	184.8	9.7	155.0	371	7.6
Dyfed	143	9.7	167.5	7.5	131.3	372	7.6
Gwent	163	11.1	189.8	9.0	161.7	358	7.2
Gwynedd	96	5.4	108.3	4.4	87.1	363	7.7
Mid Glamorgan	151	12.7	181.3	10.9	158.5	291	7.0
Powys	53	3.3	61.7	2.2	44.4	369	7.4
South Glamorgan	145	15.7	137.9	14.1	122.1	294	6.2
West Glamorgan	126	11.3	143.4	10.2	125.4	338	7.1
Wales	1,039	80.9	1174.8	67.9	985.5	338	7.2
Borders	41	3.6	49.2	2.8	39.1	371	6.5
Central Scotland	87	11.8	113.3	10.1	97.7	357	6.0
Dumfries Galloway	58	5.3	68.5	4.1	53.1	358	6.5
Fife	107	8.6	131.3	7.1	114.1	324	6.9
Grampian	192	19.2	236.0	15.6	193.5	366	6.3
Highland	71	6.6	89.5	5.2	70.5	340	6.6
Lothian	232	32.4	297.2	27.1	254.9	337	6.1
Orkney	9	0.4	10.6	0.2	7.2	365	7.8
Shetland	10	0.9	11.5	0.7	8.1	355	6.2
Strathclyde	575	71.3	733.3	61.5	639.3	279	5.9
Tayside	131	12.3	160.7	10.0	134.1	339	6.6
Western Isles	9	0.3	9.0	0.2	6.6	225	6.9
Scotland	1,530	172.7	1909.9	144.5	1618.4	315	6.2
County unknown	2	31.0	87.9	24.0	76.2	n/a	6.7
No current keeper vehicle under disposal	-	n/a	466.7	n/a	383.8	n/a	8.4
Great Britain	21,157	2306.9	25369.4	1938.1	21394.2	377	7.1

1 Using mid year 1994 population estimates.

2 Nominal: Vehicles registered at any time in 1995 are counted as age 1 year at the end of 1995,

vehicles registered in 1994 are counted as age 2 at the end of 1994, etc, etc.

Table 13 Monthly vehicle registrations: Seasonally adjusted: 1991-1995[1]

Thousands

Year	Month	Cars	of which:		Motor cycles	Goods	All vehicles
			Imported cars	Company cars			
1991	January	146.3	78.5	74.5	7.6	2.8	184.3
	February	130.6	72.6	71.8	6.4	2.4	156.8
	March	149.4	80.3	76.2	7.3	2.5	181.1
	April	127.1	70.9	70.2	7.3	2.2	152.4
	May	126.2	71.2	68.3	6.8	2.4	153.7
	June	119.7	71.0	68.1	5.8	2.3	144.7
	July	129.6	74.6	73.0	6.1	2.2	160.9
	August	147.3	74.5	66.0	6.2	2.3	174.3
	September	139.9	73.7	70.1	5.8	2.4	162.9
	October	126.5	71.2	64.2	5.3	2.5	147.2
	November	129.3	69.2	66.3	6.0	2.3	151.5
	December	128.3	66.5	64.3	5.9	2.4	151.6
	All 1991	1600.1	874.2	833.1	76.5	28.6	1921.5
1992	January	129.4	68.5	69.5	6.1	2.3	154.7
	February	122.1	68.0	64.6	5.6	2.3	147.7
	March	123.9	68.9	63.4	5.4	2.5	149.1
	April	144.2	78.0	71.2	5.6	2.2	168.5
	May	130.0	72.9	68.2	5.8	2.1	156.6
	June	130.5	73.7	66.9	5.7	2.4	157.2
	July	128.0	70.9	66.4	5.8	2.7	151.7
	August	131.2	70.6	69.0	5.2	2.4	156.8
	September	130.6	70.8	66.9	4.6	2.3	153.8
	October	134.3	73.4	71.5	4.5	2.7	157.1
	November	133.3	72.5	69.3	4.5	2.5	157.4
	December	161.6	86.4	79.7	6.6	2.4	191.1
	All 1992	1599.1	874.5	826.7	65.6	28.7	1901.8
1993	January	136.2	76.1	67.6	5.4	2.2	161.9
	February	141.7	76.9	73.4	6.0	2.5	166.6
	March	140.0	76.8	74.1	5.6	2.1	164.2
	April	143.9	78.3	75.6	5.4	2.4	168.0
	May	146.6	81.0	77.6	5.4	2.5	172.0
	June	143.6	78.9	74.2	4.9	2.7	167.9
	July	147.0	83.3	72.6	4.7	2.5	168.6
	August	154.3	86.8	79.0	4.5	2.9	179.5
	September	150.6	86.5	77.6	4.0	4.2	176.4
	October	158.4	87.7	79.0	3.7	2.5	182.7
	November	161.7	91.6	81.3	4.3	3.2	188.1
	December	152.4	87.6	78.9	4.5	3.0	178.2
	All 1993	1776.5	991.5	910.1	58.4	32.8	2074.1
1994	January	167.1	91.8	84.6	6.3	2.5	194.9
	February	161.7	92.7	82.8	6.5	2.9	189.2
	March	160.4	91.8	83.2	6.0	3.2	190.0
	April	153.4	88.2	79.7	5.5	2.8	180.2
	May	160.7	89.0	81.1	5.3	3.3	189.7
	June	165.7	93.7	85.4	4.9	3.3	194.5
	July	152.6	88.7	80.7	5.1	3.4	178.3
	August	158.4	90.0	84.5	5.0	3.6	187.4
	September	159.9	90.4	87.1	4.2	3.8	188.8
	October	154.4	88.4	82.0	4.2	4.0	181.8
	November	158.6	89.4	85.6	5.6	4.5	190.1
	December	153.5	87.0	79.5	6.0	3.9	184.0
	All 1994	1906.4	1082.1	996.4	64.6	41.1	2249.0
1995	January	157.7	92.5	85.1	5.7	4.1	189.5
	February	162.4	94.7	86.0	6.1	4.2	194.4
	March	160.5	93.0	84.6	6.2	3.8	193.3
	April	152.8	92.3	81.9	6.0	4.2	181.8
	May	162.1	95.7	85.2	6.0	3.8	194.2
	June	163.4	93.6	83.9	5.1	3.9	192.5
	July	158.7	94.3	82.3	6.3	4.6	187.6
	August	162.6	94.5	86.6	5.4	3.9	192.5
	September	159.4	93.0	82.9	4.9	3.6	189.2
	October	167.3	97.1	89.9	5.3	4.0	196.8
	November	166.1	95.6	86.9	5.8	4.2	197.0
	December	165.1	96.2	87.2	6.1	3.8	197.7
	All 1995	1938.1	1132.3	1022.4	68.9	48.0	2306.6

1. Seasonal adjustment constrained to equal actual annual totals.

Table 14 Motor Vehicles registered for the first time: 1951-1984

For detail on years 1985 - 1995 see table 10

Thousands

Year	Private and light goods[1]	Goods vehicles[1]	Motor cycles scooters and mopeds[2]	Public transport vehicles[3]	Special machines etc[4]	Other vehicles[5,6]	All vehicles
1951	136.2	84.5	133.4	7.8	34.4	17.6	413.9
1952	187.6	81.8	132.5	5.4	35.3	16.0	458.6
1953	295.1	97.2	138.6	5.0	33.5	14.1	583.5
1954	386.4	109.6	164.6	5.5	35.2	17.1	718.4
1955	500.9	153.5	185.2	5.6	39.2	22.1	906.5
1956	399.7	148.0	142.8	5.1	31.9	23.3	750.8
1957	425.4	140.5	206.1	5.0	39.8	19.9	836.7
1958	555.3	172.6	182.7	4.9	47.2	18.9	981.6
1959	645.6	191.7	331.8	5.1	49.0	29.7	1252.9
1960	805.0	225.9	256.7	6.4	42.5	32.9	1369.4
1961	742.8	220.2	212.4	6.1	46.4	31.4	1259.3
1962	784.7	192.3	140.2	5.5	42.8	26.7	1192.2
1963	1008.6	206.4	165.5	6.4	47.9	31.2	1466.0
1964	1190.6	229.3	205.1	6.5	46.1	33.6	1711.2
1965	1122.5	229.4	150.9	6.8	45.4	45.7	1600.7
1966	1065.4	227.2	109.4	6.8	48.4	36.4	1493.6
1967	1116.7	221.5	137.7	6.5	53.9	38.9	1575.2
1968	1116.9	231.7	112.0	7.1	57.0	37.2	1561.9
1969	987.4	239.6	85.4	7.1	49.3	33.0	1401.8
1969	1133.2	93.8	85.4	7.1	49.3	33.0	1401.8
1970	1248.1	85.2	104.9	7.7	48.8	30.2	1524.9
1971	1462.1	74.2	127.9	9.5	37.9	30.0	1741.6
1972	1854.8	74.9	152.5	9.8	47.6	44.1	2183.7
1973	1851.3	82.7	193.6	10.0	49.7	43.0	2230.3
1974	1399.6	68.0	189.8	7.8	45.6	39.6	1750.4
1975	1317.2	67.0	264.8	7.8	48.5	44.6	1749.9
1976	1401.8	63.9	270.6	8.7	51.8	41.2	1838.0
1977	1445.0	68.8	251.3	8.8	48.3	39.8	1862.0
1978	1745.8	79.8	225.3	9.1	50.0	41.4	2151.4
1979	1891.5	91.3	285.9	9.1	47.7	44.4	2369.9
1980	1679.2	74.7	312.7	8.8	36.7	43.5	2155.6
1980	1699.2	54.9	312.7	8.8	36.7	43.5	2155.8
1981	1643.6	39.9	271.9	7.5	32.6	34.8	2030.3
1982	1745.5	41.2	231.6	7.1	41.2	39.6	2103.9
1983	1989.1	46.6	174.5	7.3	42.1	47.9	2307.5
1984	1932.6	49.6	145.2	7.2	40.1	64.2	2238.9

1 From 1969 onwards registrations for the new October 1982 taxation
   classes have been estimated. See Notes. Figures for 1951- 1969 refer to
   previous classes. From 1980 onwards figures relate to the October 1990 taxation classes
2 Includes scooters and mopeds.
3 Includes taxis but excludes tram cars.
4 Includes trench diggers, mobile cranes, etc but excludes agricultural
   tractors on exempt licences.
5 Includes crown and exempt vehicles, three wheelers, pedestrian
   controlled vehicles, and showmen's' goods vehicles.
6 Excludes vehicles officially registered by the armed forces.

Table 15 International comparisons: Vehicle stock: 1983 and 1993

Thousands

	Cars and taxis		Goods vehicles[1]		Motor cycles etc[2]		Buses and coaches		Total	
	1983	1993	1983	1993	1983	1993	1983	1993	1983	1993
Great Britain	16,158	21,531	1,755	2,319	1,479	779	73	82	19,466	24,712
Northern Ireland	413	515	38	56	15	10	2	2	468	583
United Kingdom	16,571	22,047	1,793	2,375	1,494	789	75	84	19,934	25,295
Belgium	3,263	4,110	229	375	514 [3]	175 [3]	16	15	4,022	4,675
Denmark	1,390	1,618	231	304	209	47 [3]	8	13	1,838	1,983
France	20,600	24,020	2,810	3,618 [10]	5,150	3,060 [4]	62	42 [10]	28,622	30,740
Germany	27,600	32,652	1,511	1,590	4,266	2,800 [5]	125	71	33,502	37,113
Greece	1,073	1,959	550	790 [5]	164	388	19	23	1,806	3,160
Irish Republic	724	897 [8]	70	135	25 [8]	24	3	5	822	1,061
Italy	20,389	28,200 [7]	1,562	2,443 [7]	5,231	7,570 [6]	71	78 [7]	27,253	38,291
Luxembourg	146	209	9	15	2	7 [7]	1	1	158	232
Netherlands	4,750	5,755	346	565 [5]	756	672 [4]	12	12	5,864	7,004
Portugal	1,189	3,050	288	590 [5]	100 [3]	160 [3,4]	10	11	1,587	3,811
Spain	8,714	13,441	1,529	2,735	1,310 [3]	1,279	44	47	11,597	17,502
Austria	2,414	3,368	197	276	638	515	9	9	3,258	4,168
Croatia	..	646	..	33	..	17	..	4	..	701
Czech Republic	..	2,694	..	330	..	1,152	..	25	..	4,201
Finland	1,410	1,873	165	253	214 [3]	64 [3]	9	8	1,798	2,198
Hungary	1,258	2,092	130	238	422	158	25	22	1,835	2,509
Norway	1,383	1,633	88	319	168	161 [3,7]	15	29	1,654	2,143
Slovak Republic	..	953	..	85	..	234	..	14	..	1,285
Sweden	3,007	3,566	198	302	19 [3]	52	14	14	3,238	3,934
Switzerland	2,521	3,117	190	272	862	723 [8]	12	14	3,585	4,125
Japan	26,385	40,772	16,224	22,246	16,213	16,396	231	248	59,053	79,662
USA	126,728	146,364	36,548	47,095	5,585	4,283	586	654	169,447	198,246

1 Rigid vehicles only.
2 Includes mopeds, three-wheeled vehicles but excludes pedal cycles.
3 As at 1 August.
4 Excluding mopeds.
5 1992 data.
6 As at 1 July.
7 1991 data.
8 Vehicles with current licence only.
9 As at 30 September.
10 Vehicles less than 10 years old.

Contact point for
further information:
0171 276 8515

For further details see "International Comparisons of Transport Statistics 1970-1993", published by HMSO, price £18.

Table 16 International comparisons: Vehicles per head: 1993

Vehicles per 1000 head of population

	Cars and Taxis	Buses and Coaches	Motor Cycles[1]
Great Britain	368	2.8	14
Northern Ireland	307	1.4	6
United Kingdom	366	2.7	14
Belgium	408	1.5	17
Denmark	312	2.5	9
France	418	0.7	53
Germany	486	0.9	35
Greece	189	2.2	37
Irish Republic[2]	252	1.4	7
Italy	534	1.4	..
Luxembourg	529	2.2	18
Netherlands	378	0.8	44
Portugal	309	1.2	16
Spain	344	1.2	33
European Union	421	1.4	..
Austria	426	1.2	65
Croatia	135	0.8	2
Czech Republic	261	2.5	44
Finland	369	1.6	13
Hungary	203	2.1	15
Norway	380	6.8	37
Slovak Republic	179	2.5	44
Sweden	408	1.6	6
Switzerland	449	2.0	104
Japan	327	2.0	132
USA	568	2.5	17

1 Includes mopeds, three-wheeled vehicles but excludes pedal cycles.
2 Vehicles with current license and as at 30 September.
3 As at 1 August
4 Excluding mopeds.
5 1992 data

Table 17 International comparisons: Road goods vehicles: 1993

Thousands

	Rigid Goods Vehicles	Road Tractors	Trailers and semi trailers
Great Britain	2441	108	..
Northern Ireland	59	3	..
United Kingdom	2500	111	227
Belgium	375	39	113
Denmark [1]	304	17	363
France [2]	3,618	175	173
Germany	1,590	551	518 [6]
Greece	808	..	..
Irish Republic [3]	135	..	..
Italy	2,543 [5]	..	..
Luxembourg [3]	15	10	16 [11]
Netherlands	565	41	..
Portugal	590	16	26 [11]
Spain	2,735	77	136
European Union [4]	15,778	1,036	1,571
Austria	276	401	346
Croatia	33	2	17
Czech Republic	330	161	69
Finland	253	3	439
Hungary	238	37 [7]	242
Norway [3]	319	210	390
Slovak Republic	131	65	72
Sweden	302	4	457
Switzerland	272	6 [8]	117 [9]
Japan	22,246	100	100
USA	47,095	1,412	3,906

1 As from 1980, figures include imported second-hand vehicles.

2 Goods vehicles are those less than 10 years old.

3 Vehicles with current license only.

4 Excludes countries for which data is not available.

5 Estimated

6 Excluding two-wheeled trailers with a standard body

7 Data refers to tractors provided with road registration numbers
    including agricultural tractors

8 Heavy industrial and agricultural tractors are included under tractors

9 As from 1986, tractors for semi-trailers are included with rigid vehicles.

Table 18 Goods vehicle stock at end of year: 1985 - 1995

Thousands

| | | Articulated vehicles | | | | All |
| | | Not over | | over | | |
Year	Rigid vehicles	28 tonnes	28-37 tonnes	37 tonnes	All	vehicles
1985	341	12	52	26	90	432
1986 [1]	341	13	46	34	93	435
1987	346	14	43	41	98	444
1988	357	14	40	51	105	462
1989	368	14	36	60	110	478
1990 [1]	353	14	30	63	106	460
1991	330	13	26	61	100	430
1992	316	13	23	63	99	415
1993	313	12	21	64	98	410
1994	312	13	20	71	103	416
1995	311	13	18	76	107	418

1 The analysis was delayed until the end of January the following year. Figures therefore include vehicles
newly registered (about 3,000 in 1987 and 2,000 in 1991) or scrapped during the following January.

Trailers - analysis by axle type[1]

Thousands

National totals	1 axle	2 axle	3 axle	4 axle	5 axle	Total
First / Annual tests in 1992	13.1	132.2	75.6	0.1	-	221.0
First / Annual tests in 1993	12.0	128.5	83.7	0.1	-	224.3
First / Annual tests in 1994	11.1	122.3	92.1	0.1	-	225.6

1 This table is derived from Vehicle Inspectorate data on the number of trailers tested.
  Total stock at the end of 1991 was estimated to be between 230 and 240 thousand trailers.

Table 19 Goods vehicle stock: by gross weight and axle configuration: 1995

Thousands

Tractor	Trailer	Over Not over	3.5t 7.5t	7.5t 12t	12t 16t	16t 20t	20t 24t	24t 28t	28t 32t	32t 33t	33t 37t	37t 38t	38t	All weights
Rigid vehicles														
2 Axle			150.7	15.9	22.8	73.5	-	-	-	-	0.0	-	-	263.1
3 Axle			0.1	0.1	0.1	0.4	3.9	23.3	0.0	-	0.0	-	0.0	27.8
4 Axle			-	-	0.2	0.1	-	0.1	19.1	-	0.0	0.0	0.0	19.6
All rigid			150.8	16.0	23.1	74.0	3.9	23.4	19.1	-	0.0	-	-	310.5
Articulated vehicles														
2 Axle	2 Axle		-	0.0	-	0.1	0.4	3.6	-	-	-	-	0.0	4.2
	3 Axle		-	0.0	-	-	0.1	0.3	0.2	0.6	1.2	41.2	-	43.6
	Any		0.2	-	0.1	1.2	0.8	5.7	1.9	13.6	0.1	0.9	-	24.5
All 2 Axle			0.2	-	0.1	1.4	1.2	9.6	2.1	14.2	1.2	42.2	-	72.3
3 Axle	2 Axle		-	-	0.0	0.0	-	-	-	0.3	0.1	-	-	0.5
	3 Axle		0.0	0.0	-	-	-	-	-	0.1	0.1	18.2	0.4	18.8
	Any		-	-	-	0.1	-	0.3	-	0.1	-	14.8	0.3	15.8
All 3 Axle			-	-	-	0.1	-	0.3	0.1	0.5	0.2	33.1	0.7	35.1
2 & 3 Axle	2 Axle		-	-	-	0.1	0.4	3.7	-	0.3	0.1	0.1	-	4.7
	3 Axle		-	0.0	-	-	0.1	0.4	0.2	0.7	1.2	59.4	0.4	62.4
	Any		0.2	0.1	0.1	1.3	0.9	5.9	2.0	13.8	0.1	15.8	0.3	40.3
All articulated			0.2	0.1	0.1	1.4	1.3	10.0	2.2	14.8	1.4	75.3	0.7	107.4

Table 20 Goods vehicle stock: by taxation group and axle configuration: 1995

Thousands

Taxation class(es)	Rigid vehicles				Articulated vehicles									
					2 axle tractor				3 axle tractor					
	2 axle	3 axle	4 axle	All	2 axle trailer	3 axle trailer	any trailer	All	2 axle trailer	3 axle trailer	any trailer	All	All	All
General goods														
1 HGV	245.6	25.6	19.2	290.5	4.2	43.4	23.9	71.5	0.5	18.7	15.7	34.9	106.3	396.9
2 Trailer HGV	5.1	1.5	-	6.6	0.0	-	-	-	0.0	0.0	-	-	-	6.6
Farmers goods														
3 HGV	4.0	0.2	0.1	4.2	-	0.2	0.2	0.4	-	-	0.1	0.1	0.5	4.7
4 Trailer HGV	0.1	0.1	-	0.2	0.0	0.0	0.0	0.0	0.0	0.0	0.0	0.0	0.0	0.2
Showman's goods														
5 HGV	0.4	-	-	0.5	-	-	-	-	-	-	-	-	-	0.5
6 Trailer HGV	-	0.0	0.0	-	0.0	0.0	0.0	0.0	0.0	0.0	0.0	0.0	0.0	-
Restricted														
7 HGV	1.4	0.1	-	1.4	0.0	-	0.1	0.1	0.0	0.0	-	-	0.1	1.5
8 HGV Farmers	-	0.0	-	-	0.0	0.0	0.0	0.0	0.0	0.0	0.0	0.0	0.0	-
9 HGV showman's	0.3	0.1	0.1	0.5	0.0	-	0.2	0.2	0.0	0.0	0.1	0.1	0.2	0.7
Others														
16 Small Island	0.1	-	-	0.1	0.0	0.0	-	-	0.0	0.0	-	-	-	0.1
Electric classes	3.1	-	-	3.1	0.0	0.0	-	-	0.0	0.0	0.0	0.0	-	3.1
Crown vehicles	0.5	-	-	0.6	0.0	-	-	-	0.0	0.0	-	-	-	0.6
Exempt not crown	2.5	0.2	0.1	2.7	-	-	0.2	0.2	0.0	-	-	-	0.2	2.9
Total	263.1	27.8	19.6	310.5	4.2	43.6	24.5	72.3	0.5	18.8	15.8	35.1	107.4	418.0

1 Only vehicles in these taxation groups greater than 3500kg gross vehicle weight, and with goods vehicle body type.

Table 21 Goods vehicle stock: by gross vehicle weight and type of body: 1995

Thousands

Column headings: "Over" / "Not over" weight bands. Columns below are expressed as ranges (Over X, Not over Y).

Body type	3.5t–7.5t	7.5t–12t	12t–16t	16t–20t	20t–24t	24t–28t	28t–32t	32t–33t	33t–37t	37t–38t	38t	All weights
Rigid vehicles												
Panel Van	6.1	0.1	0.1	0.2	-	-	0.0		0.0		0.0	6.4
Box Van	57.0	6.5	7.5	23.5	0.9	1.2	0.1		0.0		0.0	96.6
Luton Van	2.6	0.3	0.5	0.3	-	-	-		0.0		0.0	3.6
Insulated Van	5.5	1.0	0.8	3.4	0.1	0.4	-		0.0		0.0	11.3
Van	3.3	0.3	0.5	0.4	-	-	-		0.0		0.0	4.5
Livestock Carrier	1.6	0.2	0.2	0.3	-	0.2	-		-		0.0	2.6
Float	3.1	-	-	-	-	-	0.0		0.0		0.0	3.2
Flat Lorry	10.5	1.7	1.9	8.1	0.6	2.1	1.1		0.0		0.0	26.0
Dropside Lorry	12.1	1.0	1.7	4.8	0.1	0.5	0.1		-		0.0	20.3
Tipper	22.8	1.2	2.8	7.8	0.2	7.5	12.4		0.0		0.0	54.6
Tanker	0.3	0.2	0.3	3.1	0.1	2.3	0.9		-		0.0	7.2
Concrete Mixer	0.1	-	0.2	0.2	-	2.7	0.1		0.0		0.0	3.3
Refuse Disposal	0.4	0.2	0.1	3.4	1.0	2.7	1.1		0.0		0.0	8.9
Goods	5.2	0.6	0.9	3.6	0.2	0.9	0.7		0.0		0.0	12.2
Skip Loader	0.9	0.1	0.2	4.7	0.1	0.5	0.6		0.0		0.0	7.1
Other or not known	19.3	2.7	5.5	10.1	0.6	2.4	1.9		0.0		-	42.5
Total	150.8	16.0	23.1	74.0	3.9	23.4	19.1		0.0		-	310.5
Articulated vehicles[1]												
Panel Van			-	-	0.0	-	-	-	0.0	-	0.0	0.1
Box Van			0.1	0.2	0.2	1.8	0.6	2.4	0.3	6.8	-	12.7
Luton Van			-	-	-	-	0.0	-	0.0	-	0.0	-
Insulated Van			-	-	-	-	-	0.3	-	1.3	-	1.8
Van			-	-	-	-	-	-	-	0.2	-	0.3
Livestock Carrier			-	0.0	-	-	-	-	-	0.1	0.0	0.1
Float			-	0.0	0.0	-	0.0	-	0.0	-	0.0	-
Flat Lorry			-	0.1	0.1	0.5	0.1	1.1	0.1	6.4	0.1	8.5
Dropside Lorry			-	-	-	-	0.0	-	-	0.2	0.0	0.2
Tipper			-	-	-	0.1	-	0.1	-	2.4	-	2.6
Tanker			-	-	-	0.2	-	0.6	-	4.0	-	4.9
Concrete Mixer			0.0	-	0.0	-	0.0	0.0	0.0	-	0.0	-
Refuse Disposal			0.0	-	0.0	-	-	0.0	0.0	-	0.0	-
Goods			-	0.3	0.2	1.7	0.2	2.6	0.2	13.4	-	18.8
Skip Loader			-	-	0.0	-	-	-	0.0	-	0.0	-
Others or not known			0.1	0.6	0.7	5.5	1.2	7.6	0.8	40.3	0.5	57.3
Total			0.3	1.4	1.3	10.0	2.2	14.8	1.4	75.3	0.7	107.4
Rigid and articulated vehicles												
Panel Van	6.1	0.1	0.1	0.2	-	-	-	-	0.0	-	0.0	6.5
Box Van	57.1	6.5	7.5	23.7	1.1	3.0	0.7	2.4	0.3	6.9	-	109.3
Luton Van	2.6	0.3	0.5	0.3	-	-	-	-	0.0	-	0.0	3.7
Insulated Van	5.5	1.0	0.8	3.4	0.1	0.4	-	0.3	-	1.3	-	13.1
Van	3.3	0.3	0.5	0.4	-	0.1	-	-	-	0.2	-	4.9
Livestock Carrier	1.7	0.2	0.2	0.3	-	0.2	-	-	-	0.1	0.0	2.7
Float	3.1	-	-	-	-	-	0.0	-	0.0	-	0.0	3.3
Flat Lorry	10.5	1.7	1.9	8.2	0.7	2.6	1.2	1.1	0.1	6.4	0.1	34.4
Dropside Lorry	12.1	1.0	1.7	4.8	0.1	0.5	0.1	-	-	0.2	0.0	20.6
Tipper	22.8	1.2	2.8	7.8	0.2	7.6	12.5	0.1	-	2.4	-	57.3
Tanker	0.3	0.2	0.3	3.1	0.1	2.5	1.0	0.6	-	4.0	-	12.1
Concrete Mixer	0.1	-	0.2	0.2	-	2.7	0.1	0.0	0.0	-	0.0	3.3
Refuse Disposal	0.4	0.2	0.1	3.4	1.0	2.7	1.1	0.0	0.0	-	0.0	9.0
Goods	5.2	0.7	0.9	4.0	0.5	2.6	0.9	2.6	0.2	13.4	-	31.0
Skip Loader	0.9	0.1	0.2	4.8	0.1	0.5	0.6	-	0.0	-	0.0	7.1
Others or not known	19.4	2.7	5.5	10.7	1.3	7.9	3.1	7.6	0.8	40.3	0.5	99.9
All body types	151.0	16.0	23.2	75.5	5.2	33.4	21.3	14.8	1.4	75.3	0.7	418.0

1 Body type normally refers to that of the trailer, or most frequently used trailer, but for about 33,000 vehicle in this group no trailer information is available and description is given only as "articulated tractor unit".

Table 22 Goods vehicle stock: by GVW [1] and year of 1st registration: 1995

Thousands

Year of first registration	Over Not over	3.5t 7.5t	7.5t 12t	12t 16t	16t 20t	20t 24t	24t 28t	28t 32t	32t 33t	33t 37t	37t 38t	38t	All weights
Rigid vehicles													
Pre 1985		20.0	2.4	26.1	7.5	0.3	2.9	1.5		-		-	38.4
1985		8.2	0.8	10.3	3.9	0.1	1.2	0.7		0.0		0.0	16.2
1986		8.8	1.0	11.4	4.4	0.2	1.4	1.1		0.0		0.0	18.4
1987		11.4	1.2	14.6	5.8	0.3	1.8	1.5		0.0		0.0	24.0
1988		15.6	1.4	19.5	8.5	0.3	2.6	2.5		0.0		0.0	33.3
1989		16.8	1.7	21.1	9.0	0.4	3.1	3.0		0.0		0.0	36.6
1990		13.6	1.5	17.3	7.0	0.4	2.1	1.4		0.0		0.0	28.2
1991		9.9	1.0	12.5	4.5	0.3	1.2	0.8		-		0.0	19.3
1992		9.7	1.2	12.4	4.4	0.3	1.1	0.7		0.0		0.0	18.9
1993		10.1	1.4	13.0	5.3	0.3	1.4	1.1		0.0		0.0	21.1
1994		12.6	1.0	15.2	6.3	0.4	2.1	2.3		0.0		0.0	26.3
1995		14.0	1.2	16.9	7.3	0.6	2.6	2.4		0.0		0.0	29.8
All years		150.8	16.0	190.0	74.0	3.9	23.4	19.1		-		-	310.5
Articulated vehicles (1)													
Pre 1985			0.1		0.2	0.1	0.6	0.1	1.2	0.1	3.2	-	5.5
1985			-		0.1	0.1	0.4	-	0.6	-	2.5	-	3.7
1986			-		0.1	0.1	0.5	-	0.7	-	3.0	-	4.4
1987			-		0.1	0.1	0.8	0.1	1.0	-	4.6	-	6.7
1988			0.1		0.2	0.1	0.9	0.1	1.6	0.1	7.5	-	10.6
1989			0.1		0.3	0.1	1.1	0.1	1.7	0.1	8.9	-	12.4
1990			0.1		0.1	0.1	0.8	0.1	1.2	0.1	5.8	-	8.4
1991			-		0.2	0.1	0.7	0.1	1.0	0.2	4.2	-	6.5
1992			-		0.1	0.1	0.8	0.2	1.0	0.1	5.3	0.1	7.6
1993			-		0.1	0.1	0.9	0.2	1.5	0.2	7.4	-	10.4
1994			-		-	0.1	1.0	0.5	1.9	0.2	10.0	0.1	14.0
1995			0.1		0.1	0.2	1.5	0.5	1.4	0.3	12.9	0.5	17.2
All years			0.6		1.4	1.3	10.0	2.2	14.8	1.4	75.3	0.7	107.4
Rigid and articulated vehicles													
Pre 1985		20.0	2.4	26.2	7.7	0.4	3.4	1.6	1.2	0.1	3.2	-	43.9
1985		8.2	0.8	10.3	3.9	0.2	1.6	0.8	0.6	-	2.5	-	19.9
1986		8.9	1.0	11.4	4.5	0.2	1.9	1.1	0.7	-	3.0	-	22.8
1987		11.4	1.2	14.6	5.9	0.3	2.6	1.6	1.0	-	4.6	-	30.7
1988		15.6	1.4	19.5	8.7	0.5	3.5	2.6	1.6	0.1	7.5	-	43.9
1989		16.9	1.7	21.1	9.3	0.6	4.3	3.1	1.7	0.1	8.9	-	49.0
1990		13.6	1.5	17.3	7.2	0.5	2.9	1.6	1.2	0.1	5.8	-	36.6
1991		9.9	1.0	12.5	4.6	0.3	1.9	0.9	1.0	0.2	4.2	-	25.7
1992		9.7	1.2	12.4	4.5	0.4	1.8	0.9	1.0	0.1	5.3	0.1	26.5
1993		10.1	1.4	13.0	5.4	0.4	2.3	1.4	1.5	0.2	7.4	-	31.5
1994		12.6	1.0	15.2	6.3	0.5	3.1	2.9	1.9	0.2	10.0	0.1	40.3
1995		14.0	1.2	16.9	7.4	0.8	4.1	2.9	1.4	0.3	12.9	0.5	47.1
All years		151.0	16.0	190.4	75.5	5.2	33.4	21.3	14.8	1.4	75.3	0.7	418.0

1 GVW: Gross vehicle weight.

Table 23 Goods vehicle stock: by year of 1st registration and type of body: 1995

Thousands

Body type	1985 & before	1986	1987	1988	1989	1990	1991	1992	1993	1994	1995	All years
Rigid vehicles												
Panel Van	0.5	0.3	0.5	0.7	0.8	0.8	0.6	0.4	0.5	0.7	0.6	6.4
Box Van	9.6	4.1	6.4	10.0	11.1	8.9	7.0	7.7	9.1	10.5	12.4	96.6
Luton Van	1.3	0.3	0.3	0.4	0.4	0.3	0.2	0.1	0.1	0.1	0.2	3.6
Insulated Van	0.9	0.5	0.6	0.8	1.0	1.2	1.1	1.3	1.1	1.2	1.5	11.3
Van	1.7	0.3	0.6	0.5	0.4	0.3	0.2	0.2	0.2	0.1	0.2	4.6
Livestock Carrier	1.2	0.2	0.2	0.2	0.2	0.2	0.1	0.1	0.1	0.1	0.1	2.6
Float	2.1	0.2	0.2	0.2	0.2	0.1	0.1	0.1	-	-	-	3.2
Flat Lorry	8.6	2.1	2.4	3.0	3.0	1.9	0.9	0.8	0.8	1.1	1.3	26.0
Dropside Lorry	4.4	1.3	1.6	2.3	2.6	1.8	0.9	0.9	1.2	1.6	1.7	20.3
Tipper	10.5	3.5	4.1	6.3	7.4	4.7	2.8	2.2	3.1	5.1	5.0	54.6
Tanker	1.3	0.5	0.7	0.9	0.8	0.6	0.6	0.4	0.3	0.4	0.6	7.2
Concrete Mixer	0.3	0.2	0.3	0.6	0.6	0.4	0.1	0.1	0.1	0.2	0.5	3.3
Refuse Disposal	0.6	0.5	0.7	1.0	1.0	1.0	0.7	0.7	0.8	0.9	1.0	8.9
Goods	2.9	1.3	1.2	1.6	1.8	1.3	0.7	0.8	0.3	0.1	0.2	12.2
Skip Loader	1.4	0.5	0.6	0.9	0.9	0.7	0.3	0.2	0.3	0.5	0.7	7.1
Total	54.6	18.4	24.0	33.3	36.6	28.2	19.3	18.9	21.1	26.3	29.8	310.5
Articulated vehicles												
Panel Van	-	-	-	-	-	-	-	-	-	-	-	0.1
Luton Van	-	-	-	0.0	-	-	-	-	0.0	0.0	-	-
Insulated Van	0.1	0.1	0.1	0.1	0.1	0.2	0.2	0.2	0.2	0.3	0.2	1.8
Van	0.1	-	-	-	-	-	-	-	-	-	-	0.3
Livestock Carrier	-	-	-	-	-	-	-	-	-	-	-	0.1
Float	-	-	-	-	0.0	-	-	-	0.0	0.0	-	-
Flat Lorry	2.1	0.6	0.8	1.1	0.9	0.6	0.4	0.4	0.4	0.5	0.7	8.5
Dropside Lorry	-	-	-	-	-	-	-	-	-	-	-	0.2
Tipper	0.3	0.2	0.2	0.3	0.3	0.2	0.1	0.1	0.2	0.3	0.4	2.6
Tanker	0.4	0.3	0.4	0.5	0.7	0.4	0.3	0.6	0.4	0.5	0.6	4.9
Concrete Mixer	-	0.0	-	-	0.0	0.0	0.0	0.0	0.0	0.0	-	-
Refuse Disposal	-	0.0	-	-	-	-	0.0	-	-	-	-	-
Goods	2.6	1.1	1.8	3.2	3.8	2.2	1.4	1.5	0.5	0.3	0.3	18.8
Skip Loader	-	-	0.0	-	-	-	-	0.0	-	-	0.0	-
Total	9.2	4.4	6.7	10.6	12.4	8.4	6.5	7.6	10.4	14.0	17.2	107.4
Rigid and articulated vehicles												
Panel Van	0.5	0.3	0.5	0.7	0.9	0.8	0.6	0.4	0.5	0.7	0.6	6.5
Box Van	10.1	4.3	6.9	11.1	12.4	9.8	7.9	8.8	10.6	12.7	14.6	109.3
Luton Van	1.3	0.3	0.3	0.4	0.4	0.3	0.2	0.1	0.1	0.1	0.2	3.7
Insulated Van	1.0	0.5	0.8	0.9	1.1	1.4	1.3	1.4	1.4	1.5	1.7	13.1
Van	1.7	0.3	0.6	0.5	0.4	0.4	0.2	0.2	0.2	0.1	0.2	4.9
Livestock Carrier	1.3	0.2	0.2	0.2	0.2	0.2	0.1	0.1	0.1	0.1	0.1	2.7
Float	2.2	0.2	0.2	0.2	0.2	0.1	0.1	0.1	-	-	-	3.3
Flat Lorry	10.7	2.7	3.2	4.1	3.9	2.5	1.3	1.2	1.2	1.6	2.1	34.4
Dropside Lorry	4.4	1.3	1.6	2.3	2.6	1.8	1.0	0.9	1.2	1.6	1.7	20.6
Tipper	10.8	3.7	4.3	6.6	7.7	4.9	2.9	2.3	3.2	5.3	5.4	57.3
Tanker	1.8	0.8	1.0	1.3	1.5	1.0	0.9	1.0	0.8	0.8	1.2	12.1
Concrete Mixer	0.3	0.2	0.3	0.6	0.6	0.4	0.1	0.1	0.1	0.2	0.5	3.3
Refuse Disposal	0.6	0.5	0.7	1.0	1.0	1.0	0.7	0.7	0.8	0.9	1.0	9.0
Goods	5.6	2.5	3.0	4.8	5.6	3.5	2.1	2.2	0.8	0.4	0.5	31.0
Skip Loader	1.5	0.5	0.6	0.9	1.0	0.7	0.3	0.2	0.3	0.5	0.7	7.1
Total	63.8	22.8	30.7	43.9	49.0	36.6	25.7	26.5	31.5	40.3	47.1	418.0

1 Body type normally refers to that of the trailer, or most frequently used trailer, but for about 33,000 vehicle in this group
no trailer information is available and description is given only as "articulated tractor unit".

Table 24 Goods vehicle stock: by county, region and axle configuration: 1995

Thousands

County/ Region/ Country	Rigid vehicles				Articulated vehicles									
					2 axle tractor				3 axle tractor					
	2 axle	3 axle	4 axle	All	2 axle trailer	3 axle trailer	any trailer	All	2 axle trailer	3 axle trailer	any trailer	All	All	All
Cleveland	1.60	0.22	0.08	1.91	0.02	0.81	0.17	0.99	0.00	0.10	0.19	0.29	1.28	3.19
Cumbria	2.10	0.35	0.18	2.64	0.05	1.01	0.15	1.21	-	0.36	0.35	0.71	1.92	4.56
Durham	2.04	0.30	0.28	2.62	0.10	0.70	0.14	0.94	-	0.16	0.23	0.39	1.33	3.95
Northumberland	0.90	0.13	0.15	1.18	0.02	0.27	0.04	0.32	0.00	0.11	0.08	0.19	0.51	1.69
Tyne and Wear	3.79	0.31	0.22	4.31	0.04	0.36	0.26	0.65	0.01	0.18	0.15	0.34	0.99	5.30
Northern	10.44	1.30	0.91	12.65	0.22	3.14	0.77	4.12	0.01	0.90	1.00	1.91	6.04	18.69
Humberside	2.74	0.39	0.23	3.36	0.06	1.37	0.19	1.62	-	0.84	0.55	1.40	3.02	6.38
North Yorkshire	4.55	0.75	0.38	5.67	0.05	1.27	0.30	1.62	-	0.43	0.32	0.75	2.37	8.04
South Yorkshire	6.40	0.62	0.48	7.50	0.11	0.96	0.61	1.68	0.01	0.39	0.58	0.98	2.66	10.16
West Yorkshire	12.00	0.89	0.55	13.44	0.18	1.84	1.12	3.14	0.03	0.64	0.72	1.39	4.54	17.98
Yorks and H'side	25.69	2.66	1.63	29.98	0.40	5.44	2.22	8.06	0.05	2.31	2.17	4.52	12.58	42.57
Derbyshire	4.11	0.53	0.53	5.17	0.01	0.65	0.38	1.04	0.01	0.28	0.26	0.55	1.59	6.77
Leicestershire	3.89	0.42	0.49	4.79	0.08	0.47	0.23	0.79	-	0.23	0.15	0.38	1.16	5.96
Lincolnshire	2.82	0.34	0.26	3.42	0.04	0.95	0.21	1.20	0.01	0.81	0.42	1.25	2.45	5.87
Northamptonshire	4.39	0.28	0.15	4.82	0.23	0.58	0.95	1.76	-	0.25	0.24	0.49	2.25	7.07
Nottinghamshire	5.20	0.67	0.42	6.29	0.05	0.71	0.53	1.29	0.01	0.24	0.32	0.57	1.85	8.14
East Midlands	20.41	2.23	1.85	24.49	0.42	3.35	2.30	6.08	0.03	1.82	1.39	3.23	9.31	33.80
Cambridgeshire	3.81	0.38	0.29	4.48	0.09	1.06	0.60	1.75	-	0.47	0.28	0.75	2.50	6.98
Norfolk	3.21	0.39	0.34	3.94	0.03	0.90	0.34	1.26	0.01	0.58	0.32	0.91	2.17	6.11
Suffolk	3.17	0.32	0.19	3.68	0.06	1.28	0.53	1.87	0.04	0.69	1.14	1.87	3.73	7.42
East	10.18	1.10	0.82	12.10	0.18	3.24	1.46	4.88	0.06	1.74	1.74	3.53	8.41	20.51
Bedfordshire	2.10	0.24	0.36	2.70	0.02	0.35	0.18	0.54	0.01	0.19	0.08	0.28	0.82	3.52
Berkshire	4.51	0.26	0.17	4.94	0.09	0.45	0.54	1.07	-	0.18	0.12	0.30	1.37	6.31
Buckinghamshire	3.64	0.41	0.37	4.41	0.07	1.63	0.47	2.17	-	0.32	0.36	0.68	2.85	7.27
East Sussex	2.16	0.13	0.10	2.39	0.01	0.12	0.04	0.18	0.00	0.09	0.02	0.11	0.29	2.68
Essex	5.96	0.67	0.71	7.34	0.05	1.26	0.42	1.73	0.02	0.67	0.36	1.05	2.78	10.12
Greater London	24.25	1.50	1.67	27.43	0.39	2.11	2.19	4.68	0.07	0.84	0.55	1.46	6.14	33.57
Hampshire	5.69	0.47	0.42	6.58	0.08	0.67	0.51	1.26	-	0.29	0.23	0.52	1.78	8.36
Hertfordshire	5.47	0.63	0.45	6.54	0.02	0.89	0.65	1.56	-	0.30	0.17	0.47	2.03	8.57
Isle of Wight	0.31	0.03	0.01	0.36	0.00	0.01	0.01	0.02	0.00	0.01	0.04	0.05	0.06	0.42
Kent	5.48	0.68	0.48	6.64	0.10	1.00	0.29	1.39	0.01	0.88	0.31	1.20	2.59	9.23
Oxfordshire	2.32	0.29	0.24	2.85	0.02	0.58	0.30	0.90	-	0.08	0.07	0.15	1.05	3.90
Surrey	5.08	0.49	0.16	5.73	0.02	0.39	0.17	0.58	-	0.10	0.06	0.16	0.74	6.47
West Sussex	2.27	0.15	0.17	2.59	0.04	0.14	0.11	0.29	0.00	0.07	0.05	0.12	0.41	3.00
South East	69.23	5.94	5.32	80.49	0.90	9.59	5.88	16.36	0.12	4.00	2.42	6.54	22.90	103.41
Avon	5.76	0.56	0.44	6.76	0.05	0.55	0.40	0.99	0.01	0.27	0.18	0.46	1.45	8.22
Cornwall	1.84	0.30	0.09	2.23	0.01	0.15	0.04	0.21	-	0.13	0.05	0.19	0.40	2.63
Devonshire	3.40	0.57	0.28	4.24	0.02	0.47	0.14	0.63	-	0.33	0.10	0.43	1.06	5.30
Dorset	1.98	0.27	0.12	2.37	0.03	0.21	0.07	0.31	0.00	0.12	0.04	0.16	0.46	2.83
Gloucestershire	1.90	0.33	0.17	2.39	0.03	0.35	0.11	0.49	-	0.18	0.09	0.27	0.76	3.16
Somerset	3.28	0.79	0.42	4.49	0.03	1.22	0.66	1.90	-	0.25	0.22	0.47	2.37	6.87
Wiltshire	3.89	0.29	0.19	4.37	0.11	0.49	0.41	1.00	0.01	0.15	0.18	0.33	1.34	5.71
South West	22.03	3.11	1.71	26.85	0.27	3.43	1.83	5.53	0.02	1.43	0.86	2.31	7.84	34.70

Table 24 (Cont'd) Goods vehicle stock: by county, region and axle configuration: 1995

Thousands

County/Region/Country	Rigid vehicles				Articulated vehicles									
					2 axle tractor				3 axle tractor					
	2 axle	3 axle	4 axle	All	2 axle trailer	3 axle trailer	any trailer	All	2 axle trailer	3 axle trailer	any trailer	All	All	All
Hereford & Worcs	3.33	0.42	0.16	3.92	0.04	0.46	0.52	1.02	0.01	0.26	0.24	0.51	1.52	5.44
Salop	2.59	0.31	0.22	3.11	0.04	0.49	0.18	0.71	-	0.28	0.19	0.48	1.18	4.29
Staffordshire	5.00	0.57	0.41	5.98	0.17	0.88	0.91	1.96	0.01	0.46	0.40	0.87	2.83	8.81
Warwickshire	2.45	0.23	0.14	2.81	0.12	0.29	0.59	1.00	-	0.24	0.17	0.41	1.41	4.22
West Midlands	20.35	2.12	1.28	23.75	0.29	2.05	1.69	4.02	0.08	0.86	0.57	1.51	5.53	29.29
West Midlands	33.72	3.65	2.20	39.57	0.66	4.17	3.89	8.71	0.10	2.10	1.57	3.77	12.48	52.05
Cheshire	4.96	0.52	0.42	5.90	0.13	1.35	0.54	2.01	0.01	0.42	0.46	0.89	2.90	8.80
Gtr Manchester	18.04	1.34	0.83	20.21	0.35	1.88	1.89	4.12	0.03	0.57	1.02	1.63	5.74	25.95
Lancashre	8.11	0.70	0.59	9.41	0.18	1.03	0.72	1.93	0.01	0.49	0.65	1.16	3.08	12.49
Merseyside	3.81	0.38	0.44	4.62	0.10	0.89	0.50	1.49	-	0.30	0.35	0.66	2.14	6.76
North Western	34.92	2.94	2.27	40.13	0.76	5.15	3.64	9.54	0.07	1.79	2.47	4.33	13.87	54.00
England	226.61	22.94	16.71	266.25	3.79	37.51	21.98	63.28	0.45	16.09	13.61	30.15	93.43	359.72
Borders	0.53	0.11	0.01	0.65	0.01	0.09	0.02	0.12	0.00	0.05	0.03	0.08	0.20	0.85
Central Scotland	1.45	0.21	0.16	1.82	0.01	0.31	0.15	0.48	0.00	0.13	0.18	0.30	0.78	2.60
Dumfries & Galloway	1.05	0.13	0.07	1.26	0.03	0.26	0.03	0.32	-	0.16	0.10	0.27	0.59	1.85
Fife	0.91	0.19	0.11	1.21	0.01	0.18	0.06	0.24	-	0.05	0.09	0.14	0.38	1.59
Grampain	2.26	0.43	0.25	2.94	0.01	0.96	0.15	1.12	-	0.43	0.18	0.61	1.73	4.67
Highland	0.94	0.19	0.08	1.21	-	0.17	0.02	0.19	0.00	0.09	0.07	0.15	0.35	1.56
Lothian	2.59	0.33	0.18	3.10	0.03	0.40	0.21	0.63	0.00	0.13	0.11	0.24	0.88	3.97
Orkney	0.14	0.05	0.01	0.19	-	-	0.01	0.01	0.00	0.01	0.01	0.01	0.03	0.22
Shetland	0.16	0.03	0.01	0.21	-	0.01	0.01	0.02	0.00	-	0.01	0.02	0.03	0.25
Strathclyde	8.42	1.08	0.67	10.17	0.04	0.98	0.47	1.49	0.01	0.49	0.65	1.14	2.63	12.80
Tayside	1.68	0.34	0.09	2.10	0.01	0.32	0.13	0.46	-	0.16	0.08	0.24	0.70	2.80
Western Isles	0.14	0.04	0.01	0.19	0.00	0.01	0.01	0.02	0.00	0.02	0.01	0.03	0.04	0.23
Scotland	20.26	3.13	1.64	25.03	0.15	3.69	1.27	5.10	0.02	1.70	1.50	3.23	8.33	33.37
Clwyd	1.63	0.25	0.26	2.14	0.04	0.37	0.25	0.66	-	0.17	0.09	0.26	0.92	3.06
Dyfed	1.84	0.30	0.12	2.25	0.03	0.29	0.04	0.36	-	0.15	0.10	0.25	0.61	2.86
Gwent	1.84	0.18	0.14	2.16	0.07	0.43	0.19	0.69	-	0.15	0.07	0.22	0.91	3.07
Gwynedd	1.05	0.12	0.10	1.26	0.01	0.05	0.02	0.08	-	0.02	0.05	0.07	0.15	1.42
Mid Glamorgan	1.64	0.19	0.19	2.02	0.04	0.29	0.13	0.46	-	0.05	0.06	0.11	0.57	2.59
Powys	0.99	0.20	0.06	1.26	0.02	0.11	0.04	0.17	-	0.07	0.03	0.10	0.26	1.52
South Glamorgan	1.57	0.12	0.09	1.77	0.01	0.17	0.06	0.24	-	0.07	0.06	0.13	0.37	2.14
West Glamorgan	0.99	0.09	0.07	1.15	0.01	0.10	0.05	0.17	0.00	0.06	0.05	0.11	0.28	1.43
Wales	11.55	1.44	1.02	14.01	0.22	1.81	0.79	2.82	0.02	0.73	0.51	1.25	4.07	18.08
County unknown	0.70	0.07	0.02	0.79	-	0.15	0.05	0.20	-	0.05	0.04	0.10	0.30	1.09
No current keeper vehicle under disposal	3.98	0.26	0.21	4.45	0.05	0.43	0.41	0.89	0.01	0.21	0.16	0.38	1.27	5.72
Great Britain	263.09	27.84	19.61	310.53	4.21	43.58	24.50	72.29	0.50	18.78	15.82	35.10	107.39	417.97

49

Table 25 Goods vehicle stock at end of year: 1984-1994: by year of 1st registration

Thousands

Year of 1st registration	1985	1986	1987	1988	1989	1990	1991	1992	1993	1994	1995
Rigid vehicles											
Pre 1977	55.1										
1977	19.9	54.0	61.6								
1978	29.5	23.6		71.4	73.8						
1979	41.0	35.4	30.3			62.9	57.6				
1980	35.8	32.3	28.7	24.1				57.9	63.7		
1981	28.0	26.2	24.2	21.4	18.4					71.0	73.0
1982	28.7	27.7	26.3	24.4	21.7	17.5					
1983	32.8	32.1	31.3	29.7	27.4	23.4	19.4				
1984	35.1	34.6	34.1	33.1	30.9	27.4	23.5	20.5			
1985	35.6	36.4	36.1	35.2	33.9	31.2	28.1	25.1	22.4		
1986		38.8	36.4	35.8	34.7	33.2	30.5	28.0	25.4	22.8	
1987			37.6	37.8	37.3	35.9	34.2	32.2	30.4	28.3	24.0
1988				44.0	44.5	43.1	41.5	39.8	38.1	36.0	33.3
1989					45.1	44.8	43.4	42.2	41.2	39.3	36.6
1990						33.8	31.6	31.2	30.8	29.7	28.2
1991							20.0	20.2	20.2	19.6	19.3
1992								19.1	19.7	19.2	18.9
1993									20.6	21.1	21.1
1994										25.5	26.3
1995											29.8
All years	341.3	341.1	346.5	357.0	367.6	353.3	329.9	316.2	312.5	312.4	310.5
Articulated vehicles											
Pre 1977	5.0										
1977	4.3	5.9	8.7								
1978	7.9	5.8		11.5	11.5						
1979	11.6	9.3	7.7			9.4	8.9				
1980	9.1	7.8	6.6	5.2				9.5	10.8		
1981	7.8	7.0	6.2	5.2	3.9					13.2	13.6
1982	9.4	9.0	8.3	7.4	6.1	4.4					
1983	10.6	10.3	9.9	9.1	7.8	6.0	4.4				
1984	11.9	11.7	11.5	11.0	10.1	8.4	6.7	5.6			
1985	12.8	12.8	12.7	12.3	11.7	10.5	8.7	7.5	6.0		
1986		13.7	12.6	12.4	11.8	11.0	9.7	8.6	7.1	6.1	
1987			13.9	14.0	13.6	12.8	11.9	11.0	9.7	8.6	6.7
1988				16.7	16.7	16.2	15.4	14.6	13.3	12.4	10.6
1989					17.2	16.8	16.3	15.9	14.7	13.9	12.4
1990						11.1	10.2	10.1	9.5	9.2	8.4
1991							7.4	7.4	7.2	6.9	6.5
1992								8.5	8.4	8.1	7.6
1993									10.7	10.8	10.4
1994										14.0	14.0
1995											17.2
All years	90.4	93.5	97.9	104.6	110.4	106.5	99.7	98.7	97.5	103.3	107.4
Rigid and articulated vehicles											
Pre 1977	60.1										
1977	24.2	59.9	70.3								
1978	37.4	29.3		82.9	88.1						
1979	52.6	44.8	37.9			72.3	66.4				
1980	44.9	40.1	35.2	29.3				67.4	74.5		
1981	35.8	33.2	30.4	26.6	22.3					84.2	86.6
1982	38.0	36.7	34.6	31.8	27.7	21.9					
1983	43.4	42.4	41.2	38.8	35.2	29.4	23.9				
1984	47.0	46.4	45.5	44.0	41.0	35.8	30.3	26.0			
1985	48.4	49.2	48.7	47.5	45.5	41.7	36.8	32.6	28.5		
1986		52.5	48.9	48.2	46.5	44.2	40.2	36.6	32.6	28.8	
1987			51.4	51.7	50.9	48.7	46.1	43.2	40.2	36.9	30.7
1988				60.7	61.2	59.3	56.9	54.4	51.4	48.4	43.9
1989					62.3	61.6	59.8	58.1	55.9	53.2	49.0
1990						44.8	41.8	41.3	40.3	38.9	36.6
1991							27.4	27.6	27.4	26.5	25.7
1992								27.6	28.0	27.4	26.5
1993									31.3	31.9	31.5
1994										39.5	40.3
1995											47.1
All years	431.7	434.6	444.4	461.6	478.0	459.7	429.6	414.9	410.1	415.7	418.0

Table 26 Goods vehicle stock at end of year: 1985-1995: by gross vehicle weight

Thousands

Over	Not over	1985	1986	1987	1988	1989	1990	1991	1992	1993	1994	1995
Rigid vehicles												
3.5t	7.5t	146.9	150.8	155.0	161.9	169.5	166.2	157.8	152.0	151.4	150.2	150.8
7.5t	12t	29.3	26.4	24.9	23.3	22.0	20.1	18.5	17.2	16.6	15.9	16.0
12t	16t	42.8	39.2	36.7	34.5	32.2	29.2	26.0	24.3	23.5	22.7	23.1
16t	20t	78.5	80.1	82.8	86.7	89.9	87.1	80.9	77.9	75.6	75.7	74.0
20t	24t	0.9	1.0	1.4	1.8	2.1	2.4	2.5	2.7	3.0	3.4	3.9
24t	28t	25.6	25.6	26.2	27.2	28.3	26.6	24.5	23.3	23.2	24.0	23.4
28t	32t	17.2	17.9	19.4	21.6	23.5	21.5	19.5	18.6	18.5	19.9	19.1
32t		0.1	0.1	0.1	0.1	0.2	0.2	0.2	0.2	0.6	0.6	0.0
All weights		341.3	341.1	346.5	357.0	367.6	353.3	329.9	316.2	312.5	312.4	310.5
Articulated vehicles												
3.5t	16t	0.6	0.6	0.5	0.5	0.5	0.5	0.4	0.3	0.3	0.3	0.4
16t	20t	4.5	4.1	3.7	3.1	2.8	2.4	2.1	1.9	1.7	1.5	1.4
20t	24t	1.0	1.1	1.1	1.1	1.0	1.1	1.0	1.1	1.1	1.2	1.3
24t	28t	6.3	7.3	8.4	9.1	9.7	9.7	9.2	9.3	9.3	9.6	10.0
28t	32t	1.8	1.5	1.3	1.1	1.1	0.9	0.9	1.0	1.1	1.7	2.2
32t	33t	48.7	43.7	40.5	37.3	33.5	28.1	23.2	19.9	18.1	17.0	14.8
33t	37t	1.2	1.3	1.3	1.2	1.5	1.4	1.5	1.7	1.5	1.3	1.4
37t	38t	26.3	33.9	41.2	51.1	60.3	62.5	61.3	63.5	64.4	70.4	75.3
38t		-	-	-	-	-	-	-	-	-	0.2	0.7
All weights		90.4	93.5	97.9	104.6	110.4	106.5	99.7	98.7	97.5	103.3	107.4
Rigid and articulated vehicles												
3.5t	7.5t	147.2	151.0	155.3	162.1	169.8	166.4	158.1	152.2	151.6	150.4	151.0
7.5t	12t	29.5	26.6	25.1	23.4	22.1	20.2	18.5	17.2	16.6	16.0	16.0
12t	16t	42.9	39.3	36.8	34.6	32.4	29.3	26.1	24.4	23.6	22.8	23.2
16t	20t	82.9	84.2	86.4	89.8	92.6	89.5	83.0	79.8	77.2	77.2	75.5
20t	24t	2.0	2.1	2.5	2.8	3.1	3.4	3.5	3.8	4.1	4.6	5.2
24t	28t	31.9	32.9	34.5	36.3	38.1	36.3	33.7	32.7	32.5	33.5	33.4
28t	32t	19.0	19.4	20.7	22.7	24.6	22.4	20.4	19.5	19.6	21.6	21.3
32t	38t	76.2	79.0	83.1	89.7	95.5	92.2	86.2	85.3	84.6	89.2	91.5
38t		0.1	-	-	-	-	-	-	-	-	0.2	0.4	0.7
All weights		431.7	434.6	444.4	461.6	478.0	459.7	429.6	414.9	410.1	415.7	417.9

51

Table 27 Goods vehicles stock at end of year: 1990-1995: by gross vehicle weight, axle configuration

Thousands

	Gross weight Over Not over	3.5 7.5	7.5 12	12 16	16 20	20 24	24 28	28 32	32 33	33 37	37 38	38 —	All weights
Axles	Year												
Rigid vehicles													
2 Axle	1990	167.5	20.2	30.1	85.1	-	-	-	-	-	-	-	302.9
	1991	160.3	18.5	26.7	79.1	0.1	0.3	0.2	-	-	-	-	285.2
	1992	155.3	17.2	25.0	76.9	0.1	0.3	0.2	-	-	-	-	275.0
	1993	151.3	16.6	23.5	75.4	0.1	0.2	0.2	0.2	0.3	-	0.2	268.0
	1994	150.1	15.9	22.6	75.3	0.1	0.2	0.1	0.2	0.2	0.0	0.2	264.9
	1995	150.7	15.9	22.8	73.5	-	-	-	-	0.0	-	-	263.1
3 Axles	1990	0.1	-	0.1	0.3	2.3	25.6	-	-	-	-	-	28.4
	1991	0.1	-	0.1	0.3	2.4	23.5	-	-	-	-	-	26.4
	1992	0.1	-	-	0.2	2.7	22.9	-	-	-	-	-	26.0
	1993	0.1	-	-	0.2	2.9	22.8	-	-	-	-	-	26.1
	1994	0.1	0.0	0.0	0.4	3.3	23.6	0.0	0.0	0.0	0.0	0.0	27.5
	1995	0.1	0.1	0.1	0.4	3.9	23.3	0.0	-	0.0	-	0.0	27.8
4 Axles	1990	-	-	-	-	-	0.2	20.6	-	-	-	-	20.8
	1991	-	-	-	-	-	0.2	18.6	-	-	-	-	18.8
	1992	-	-	-	-	-	0.2	18.3	-	-	-	-	18.5
	1993	-	-	-	-	-	0.1	18.3	-	-	-	-	18.5
	1994	0.0	0.0	0.0	0.0	0.0	0.2	19.7	0.0	0.0	0.0	0.0	20.0
	1995	-	-	0.2	0.1	-	0.1	19.1	-	0.0	0.0	0.0	19.6
All	1990	167.6	20.2	30.2	85.4	2.5	26.2	20.9	-	-	-	-	353.0
	1991	160.4	18.6	26.8	79.3	2.6	24.0	18.8	-	-	-	-	330.5
	1992	155.4	17.3	25.0	77.1	2.8	23.4	18.5	-	-	-	-	319.5
	1993	151.4	16.6	23.5	75.6	3.0	23.2	18.5	0.2	0.3	-	0.2	312.5
	1994	150.2	15.9	22.7	75.7	3.4	24.0	19.9	0.2	0.2	0.0	0.2	312.4
	1995	150.8	16.0	23.1	74.0	3.9	23.4	19.1	-	0.0	-	-	310.5
Articulated vehicles													
2 Axle	1990		0.5		2.3	1.0	9.0	0.8	26.1	1.2	34.8	-	75.7
tractive	1991		0.4		2.0	1.0	8.8	0.7	21.3	1.3	33.5	-	69.0
units	1992		0.3		1.8	1.0	8.8	0.9	18.4	1.5	34.8	-	67.5
	1993		0.3		1.7	1.1	9.1	1.1	17.7	1.3	35.9	-	68.3
	1994	0.2	0.0	0.1	1.5	1.2	9.4	1.7	16.6	1.1	39.2	0.0	71.0
	1995	0.2	-	0.1	1.4	1.2	9.6	2.1	14.2	1.2	42.2	-	72.3
3 Axles	1990		-		-	-	0.1	-	0.3	0.2	25.3	-	25.8
tractive	1991		-		-	-	0.1	-	0.3	0.2	25.1	-	25.7
units	1992		-		-	-	0.2	-	0.3	0.2	26.7	-	27.3
	1993		-		-	-	0.2	-	0.4	0.2	28.5	-	29.3
	1994	0.0	0.0	0.0	0.0	0.0	0.1	0.0	0.4	0.2	31.2	0.2	32.3
	1995	-	-	-	0.1	-	0.3	0.1	0.5	0.2	33.1	0.7	35.1
All	1990		0.5		2.3	1.0	9.1	0.8	26.4	1.3	60.1	-	101.5
	1991		0.4		2.0	1.0	8.9	0.7	21.6	1.5	58.6	-	94.7
	1992		0.3		1.9	1.0	8.9	0.9	18.6	1.6	61.5	-	94.8
	1993		0.3		1.7	1.1	9.3	1.1	18.1	1.5	64.4	-	97.5
	1994	0.2	0.0	0.1	1.5	1.2	9.6	1.7	17.0	1.3	70.4	0.2	103.3
	1995	0.2	0.1	0.1	1.4	1.3	10.0	2.2	14.8	1.4	75.3	0.7	107.4

Notes and Definitions

1. NOTES ON THE VEHICLE INFORMATION DATABASE

1.1 The results in this publication are produced from a Vehicle Information Database (VID), held in the Department of Transport's Statistics Directorate and updated quarterly using information supplied by DVLA. The results conform to the same definitions as earlier vehicle censuses, but, for technical reasons, are considered slightly more reliable than earlier estimates.

1.2 Some vehicles have complicated licensing histories, that may include incidents such as cheques failing to clear, changes of taxation status, late payments, and one or more valid or invalid refund claims. The VID undertakes a more detailed examination of licensing history than earlier vehicle census analyses and is therefore able to provide better estimates of licensed stock.

2. NOTES ON CURRENTLY LICENSED STOCK STATISTICS: TABLES 1 to 8

Effects of using the Vehicle Information Database

2.1 The net effect of the change to the VID as the main source of statistics on currently licensed stock was to produce a small reduction - of the order of 1% - in the estimated levels of licensed stock. A number of main tables showing time series of licensed stock have therefore been broken at 1992, and show both the series based on previous census analyses up to 1992, and a series from 1992 taken from the VID. Estimates of changes between years before and after 1992 can be made by combining the changes from the two series.

Census methods used in earlier publications

2.2 Censuses based entirely on the record of licensed vehicles at DVLA began on 31 December 1978, and subsequent counts have been taken on the last day of the year up to and including 31st December 1992. There are two important differences between the censuses based entirely on DVLA records and censuses prior to 1978.

2.4 Firstly, censuses derived from DVLA records were based on a single point (one day) in time. In previous censuses, for purely administrative reasons, counts of licensed vehicles at Local Taxation Offices included any vehicle licensed for at least one month during the third quarter of the year.

2.5 Secondly, the DVLA-based censuses relied on a complete count of all vehicles, subject only to the complexities of establishing accurately the licensing status of the vehicle, whereas before 1978, information on vehicle stock had been obtained from samples.

Taxation class changes

2.6 There have been three major changes in recent years. Firstly, as from 1 October 1982, all general goods vehicles less than 1,525 kgs unladen weight were assessed for vehicle excise duty at the same rate as private vehicles, and the old "private car and van" taxation class was replaced by the new "Private and Light Goods" (PLG) taxation class. In addition, goods vehicles greater than 1,525 kgs unladen weight were to be taxed with reference to their gross vehicle weight and axle configuration, as opposed to unladen weight as in previous years. Farmers' light goods vehicles and showmen's light goods vehicles, i.e. vehicles of less than 1,525 kgs unladen weight, were allocated to their own distinct taxation classes and were not included in the PLG taxation class.

2.7 Secondly, from 1 October 1990, goods vehicles less than 3,500 kgs gross vehicle weight were transferred from the "Goods Vehicle" taxation class to the "Private and Light Goods" class. Farmers' and showmen's goods vehicles of less than 3,500 kgs gross vehicle weight, but more than 1,525 kgs unladen weight, were transferred to the "Light Goods Farmers' and "Light Goods Showmen's" taxation classes.

2.8 Finally 1995 saw major reforms of the vehicle taxation system. The bulk of the 1995 changes came into operation on 1st July 1995, but some additional changes were introduced on 29th November 1995. Full details are given in the special supplement at the start of this report.

Correction for taxation class changes

2.9 The changes described above created discontinuities in the time series for vehicles currently licensed. To correct for these discontinuities, retrospective estimates of "Private and Light Goods" and "Goods" have been made for the years before 1991 using the assumption that all general goods vehicles of less than 3,500 kgs gross vehicle weight would have been taxed as "Private and Light Goods". Private cars taxed within "Private and Light Goods" have been estimated pro-rata on the basis of information on the proportion of cars within "Private and Light Goods" available for the first time in 1983.

2.10 Between 1978 and 1982, the distribution of private cars, within "Private and Light Goods", by engine capacity has been estimated pro-rata by allocating retrospective estimates for total private cars within "Private and Light Goods" across previous distributions of "private cars and vans" by engine capacity.

2.11 As described in paragraph 2.6 above, since October 1982 gross vehicle weight has been the basis of taxation for goods vehicles. Analyses of the stock of goods vehicles by gross weight have been compiled since the 1983 census. Pre-1983 time series analysed by gross vehicle weight are not available.

2.12 The 1995 changes are not expected to have any major impact on the total number of vehicles taxed within the PLG group, and the PLG series has not been subject to any retrospective adjustment or recalculation. Retrospective series have been estimated for the new "bus" taxation class and are included in the tables.

Regional analysis

2.13 The only regional information easily obtainable from vehicle records held on computer by DVLA is the post code of the registered keeper of the vehicle. This can be used to determine the county in which the keeper lives. The county and regional analyses throughout this report have been compiled in this way. Vehicles under disposal are those where the previous owner has sold the vehicle and notified DVLA, but the new keeper has not completed and returned his part of the registration document. For such vehicles the post code of the registered keeper is unknown.

3. NOTES ON VEHICLES REGISTERED FOR THE 1ST TIME: TABLES 10 to 13

Sources

3.1 The statistics in this section are based on a complete analysis of new registrations and not on a sample count. Monthly analyses are compiled from the records of the Driver and Vehicle Licensing Agency (DVLA) by its Information Technology contractor, and forwarded to the Department of Transport's Statistics Directorate.

Correction for taxation class changes

3.2 To correct for taxation class changes, as described under sections 3.6 and 3.7 above, retrospective estimates of "Private and Light Goods" and "General Goods" were made for 1969 to 1982 by assuming that all "general goods" vehicles less than 1,525 kgs unladen vehicle weight would have been registered as PLG prior to 1 October 1982, if that taxation class had been in operation. A second set of retrospective estimates was made for 1980 to 1990 assuming that general goods vehicles of less than 3,500 kgs gross weight would have been registered as PLG.

3.3 From 1975 onwards, estimates have been made of the number of private cars taxed within the "Private and Light Goods" class. Up to 1982 general goods vehicles and Farmers' goods were taxed on their unladen weight and analyses were produced on this basis. Since 1983 gross vehicle weight has been the basis of taxation and new registrations have been analysed by gross vehicle weight.

3.4 Changes to the vehicle taxation system in 1995 will see vehicles register under the new structure from 1st July 1995. Future publications will reflect these changes and some time series will contain unavoidable discontinuities. However, time series for some individual tax classes may still be available even where the calls has been allocated to a different taxation group. For example, agricultural tractors, previously part of the "agricultural and special machines" group, now fall into the "special concessionary" group. See table 11.

4. NOTES ON HISTORIC SERIES: TABLES 9 AND 14

Motor vehicles currently licensed: census methods

4.1 Up to 1974, the figures for motor vehicles currently licensed were compiled from information received by the Department of Transport from all registration/licensing authorities or Local Taxation Offices (County, County Borough and Borough Councils) in Great Britain which administered the Vehicles (Excise) Act 1971.

4.2 Since October 1974, all new vehicles have been registered at the Driver and Vehicle Licensing Agency (DVLA), and records for older vehicles have also been transferred there, the process being completed in March 1978. For 1975 and 1976 the census was based on a combination of records held at Local Taxation Offices and at DVLA. Because of the closure of Local Taxation Offices it was not possible to produce census results in 1977. This system was superseded by censuses based entirely on the record of licensed vehicles at DVLA on 31 December 1978. Differences between censuses based entirely on DVLA records and those prior to 1978 are described in sections 3.4 and 3.5.

4.3 These differences produce a discontinuity in the stock figures in 1978. Pre-1978 figures have therefore been adjusted to make them comparable with those for later years. These adjustments have been applied after the estimation described under "correction for taxation class changes".

Correction for taxation class changes

4.4 The changes described above under 3.6 and 3.7 created a discontinuity in the time series for vehicles currently licensed. To correct for this discontinuity, retrospective estimates of "Private and Light Goods" and "Goods" have been made for the years 1950 to 1982, using the assumption that all general goods vehicles of less than 3,500 kgs gross vehicle weight would have been taxed as "Private and Light Goods" if this class had existed prior to 1983. Private cars taxed within "Private and Light Goods" have been estimated pro-rata on the basis of information on the proportion of cars within "Private and Light Goods" available for the first time in 1983.

4.5 The "Goods" category retains Farmers' goods vehicles and showmen's goods vehicles of less than 1,525 kgs unladen weight. From 1983, retrospective counts of vehicles within the new taxation class groupings were produced. Other taxation classes were unaffected by the change in goods vehicle taxation.

Motor vehicles registered for the first time

4.6 Statistics in this table are based on a complete analysis of new registrations and not on a sample count. In the past these were obtained from monthly returns of licensing authorities' records of new registrations. On 1 October 1974 the Driver and Vehicle Licensing Centre (DVLC) at Swansea took over responsibility for the licensing of vehicles from Local Taxation Offices (LTO). Initially, DVLC dealt only with new registrations, but from 1 April 1975 they began to take on the registration of older vehicles from the Local Vehicle Licensing Offices, which replaced the LTOs. On 1 April 1990, DVLC became the Driver and Vehicle Licensing Agency (DVLA).

Correction for taxation class changes

4.7 To correct for taxation class changes, retrospective estimates of "Private and Light Goods" and "General Goods" have been made for 1951 to 1982 by assuming that all "general goods" vehicles less than 3,500 kgs gross vehicle weight would have been registered as "Private and Light Goods" prior to 1 October 1982, if that taxation class had been in operation. The "Goods Vehicles" taxation class retains Farmers' goods vehicles and showmen's goods vehicles less than 1,525 kgs unladen weight. From 1975 onwards, estimates have been made of the number of private cars taxed within the "Private and Light Goods" class. Other taxation classes were unaffected by the change in goods vehicle taxation.

5. NOTES ON GOODS VEHICLE STATISTICS: TABLES 18 TO 27

5.1 The purpose of tables 18 to 27 is to provide detailed information on heavy goods vehicles in terms of their GVW and axle configuration. This population of vehicles at the end of 1995 amounts to some 418,000 vehicles, compared with 421,000 vehicles in goods vehicle taxation groups. This is a smaller difference than in some earlier reports and reflects the abolition of specialised goods taxation classes containing vehicles not more than 3500 kgs gross weight.

Goods vehicles statistics in this publication

5.2 The goods vehicle statistics provided in tables 18 onwards cover those goods vehicles over 3.5 tonnes gross vehicle weight (GVW), in taxation groups 1 - 9, that is HGV, trailer HGV and restricted HGV taxation groups for general goods, Showman's goods and Farmer's goods and class 16 small island goods vehicles. Once the 1995 changes are complete only classes 01-HGV, 02-Trailer HGV and 16-small island goods will remain active. In addition, results include vehicles in electric taxation class, crown vehicles, and vehicles with various forms of exemption, provided they exceed 3.5 tonnes gross vehicle weight have goods vehicle body type and comply with appropriate axle and weight limit regulations. Further information on taxation groups is given in table 3.

Goods vehicle statistics in earlier publications

5.3 Previous publications of "Goods Vehicles In Great Britain" were based primarily on results taken from the Goods Vehicle List (GVL), a register of vehicles over 3.5 tonnes gross weight licensed to carry goods on the public road network, and maintained by the DVLA. This list is a count of goods vehicles (greater than 3.5 tonnes gross weight) designed to provide a sampling population for the Continuing Survey of Road Goods Transport (CSRGT). However, some tables in that publication were drawn from the "Goods Vehicle Census", as described below.

5.4 Following the Armitage inquiry, the maximum weight limit for articulated vehicles was increased from 32.5 tonnes gross vehicle weight (GVW) to 38 tonnes GVW, effective from 1 May 1983. To monitor the effect of this change the Goods Vehicle Census, a new source of information on goods vehicles greater than 3.5 tonnes GVW and 1,525 kgs unladen weight (ULW), was developed based on the DVLA register. It was designed to produce detailed information on heavy goods vehicles in terms of their GVW and axle configuration. This census included goods vehicles in a wider range of tax classes than the Goods Vehicle List, including certain goods vehicles in exempt classes.

5.5 Earlier editions of "Goods Vehicles In Great Britain" explained how it was possible to reconcile the alternative estimates of goods vehicle stock provided by the two sources. After allowing for the differences in coverage the two estimates are close, the differences being attributable to the timing of the counts. The Goods Vehicle Census is taken six weeks after the end of the year census day to allow for the processing lag between application for licence and entry into the register. The GVL counts are taken on the last day of each calendar quarter since timely counts are needed for the CSRGT. Because of its use in sampling active vehicles the GVL contains recently unlicensed vehicles which may be in the process of relicensing.

6. TAXATION CLASS DEFINITIONS

Exempt vehicles

6.1 The exempt vehicles includes a number of distinct sub-groups and classes, of which the most important are:-

    Emergency vehicles.
    Crown vehicles.
    Disabled driver and disabled passenger carrying vehicles.

Vehicles previously in PLG, motorcycle or tricycle tax groups now over 25 years of age. Personal export and direct export vehicles.

The emergency vehicles group was created from 1st July 1995. These vehicles are required to obtain and display an annual tax disk but pay a nil rate of duty. Similarly exempt vehicles over 25 years of age are still required to obtain and display an annual tax disk but pay a nil rate of duty.

6.2 Vehicles owned by Government Departments and operated under Certificates of Crown ownership (apart from those belonging to the Armed Forces) are registered but exempt from vehicle excise duty.

6.3 The exempt vehicle statistics exclude cars and motor cycles used temporarily in Great Britain before being privately exported under the personal export and direct export schemes by non-United Kingdom citizens.

General haulage

6.4 General haulage vehicles may not be used for carrying loads or transporting goods except on the trailer which it is towing, where, unlike articulated heavy goods vehicles, the trailer does not form an integral part of vehicles. Many vehicles taxed for general haulage are agricultural tractors.

Goods vehicles

6.5 Goods vehicles over 3,500 kgs gross vehicle weight. Now limited to two main groups, class 01 for heavy goods vehicles, and class 02 for goods vehicles paying additional trailer duty. Goods vehicles on certain off-shore islands may qualify to tax in class 16-small island goods.

Motorcycles, scooters and mopeds

6.6 No distinction between these different types of machine is made for taxation purposes. The vehicle excise duty payable depends upon the engine capacity of the bike.

Private and light goods

6.7 Includes all vehicles used privately. The bulk of this group consists of private cars (whether owned by individuals or companies) and vans and light goods vehicles. The group also contains a number of important minority groups including private buses and coaches, private heavy goods vehicles, and some vehicles which before 1st July 1995 were taxed in specialised taxation class but which do not exceed 3500 kgs gross weight and now fall into the PLG group. A substantial number of motorcars are now taxed in the exempt disabled driver class.

6.8 A new class "Private HGV" was introduced from 29th November 1995 for heavy goods vehicles used unladen, privately or for driver training purposes. The annual duty is a flat rate £150 the basic minimum rate for HGVs.

Public transport vehicles

6.9 All vehicles classified for taxation purposes as class 34 - Bus. These are vehicles used for public conveyance, with more than 8 seats. Buses and coaches not licensed for public conveyance, and operated and used privately, are excluded and are classified for excise licensing with private and light goods. Taxis and private hire cars are now included in the private and light goods group and are not separately identified within the VED taxation system. Regulation and control of taxis and private hire cars is through local authorities who issue appropriate hackney and hire car plates.

Special concessionary group

6.10 This group of vehicles pays VED at the rate of £35 per annum and, in common with the former "agricultural and special machines" group includes agricultural tractors, combine harvesters and mowing machines. This taxation class also electric vehicles, gritting vehicles and snow ploughs, and steam powered vehicles. However, works trucks, mobile cranes and digging machines previously in the "agricultural and special machines" group are no longer included.

Special machines

6.11 This group consists of vehicles over 3500 kgs, which do not pay VED as heavy goods vehicles nor qualify for taxation in the special concessionary group. Vehicles in this group pay VED at the basic minimum rate for HGVs. Types include road rollers, works trucks and showman's vehicles.

Three wheelers

6.12 Mainly three-wheeled cars and vans not exceeding 450 kgs unladen weight. Motorised tricycles are also included but motorcycle combinations are included with motor cycles.

Trade licences

6.13 These are issued to manufacturers and repairers of, and dealers in, motor vehicles but as they do not relate to particular vehicles they are not included in any of the tables relating to current licences or new registrations.

Vehicles owned by the Armed Forces

6.14 Vehicles officially belonging to the Armed Forces, except for a small number which for particular reasons, are licensed in the ordinary way, operate under a special registration and licensing system operated by them. Such vehicles are excluded from vehicle registration figures.

Symbols and conventions

.. = not available	- = negligible (less than half the final digit shown)
0 = nil (that is exactly zero)	⎮ = change or break in the series (cf. table 2)